أعوذ بالله من الشيطان الرجيم

بسم الله الرحمن الرحيم

اللَّهُمَّ صَلِّ عَلَى سَيِّدِنَا مُحَمَّدٍ مَا اخْتَلَفَ الْمَلَوَانِ وَتَعَاقَبَ الْعَصْرَانِ وَكَرَّ الْجَدِيدَانِ وَاسْتَقَلَّ الْفَرْقَدَانِ وَبَلِّغْ رُوحَهُ وَأَرْوَاحَ أَهْلِ بَيْتِهِ مِنَّا التَّحِيَّةَ وَالسَّلَامَ وَبَارِكْ وَسَلِّمْ عَلَيْهِ كَثِيرًا.

اللَّهُمَّ صَلِّ عَلَى بَدْرِ التَّمَامِ
اللَّهُمَّ صَلِّ عَلَى نُورِ الظَّلَامِ
اللَّهُمَّ صَلِّ عَلَى مِفْتَاحِ دَارِ السَّلَامِ
اللَّهُمَّ صَلِّ عَلَى الشَّفِيعِ فِي جَمِيعِ الْأَنَامِ

يَا إِمَامَ الرُّسُلِ وَيَا سَنَدِي
أَنْتَ بَابُ اللهِ وَمُعْتَمَدِي
فَبِدُنْيَايَ وَبِآخِرَتِي

يَا رَسُولَ اللهِ خُذْ بِيَدِي
يَا حَبِيبَ اللهِ خُذْ بِيَدِي
يَا نَبِيَّ اللهِ خُذْ بِيَدِي
يَا نُورَ اللهِ خُذْ بِيَدِي

وَفِينَا رَسُولُ اللهِ يَتْلُو كِتَابَهُ
إِذَنْ شَقَّ مَعْرُوفٌ مِنَ الْفَجْرِ سَاطِعُ-

أَرَانَا الْهُدَى بَعْدَ الْعَمَى فَقُلُوبُنَا
بِهِ مُوقِنَاتٌ أَنَّ مَا قَالَ وَاقِعُ-

يَبِيتُ يُجَافِي جَنْبَهُ عَنْ فِرَاشِهِ
إِذَا اسْتَثْقَلَتْ بِالْمُشْرِكِينَ الْمَضَاجِعُ
إِذَا اسْتَثْقَلَتْ بِالْكَافِرِينَ الْمَضَاجِعُ

بشائر الخيرات وبلوغ المسرات

THE PRAYER *of* JOYOUS TIDINGS

The Ṣalawāt of Shaykh ʿAbd al-Qādir al-Jīlānī

This blessed translation, *The Ṣalawāt of ʿAbd al-Qādir al-Jīlānī*, was commissioned firstly in Rabīʿ al-Thānī of this 1447 Hijri year, the year that marks fifteen centuries since the blessed birth of the Messenger of Allah ﷺ. It was undertaken by the servant of Allah and of His Beloved ﷺ, Aḥmad Ḥabīb, as a humble gift of love, remembrance, and longing for nearness to the Beloved ﷺ and the Awliyāʾ.

These pages are placed at the threshold of our legacy, as a small gift carried upon immense meaning. They stand as a sign of devotion to the Chosen One ﷺ and to the path of those who preserved his light through hearts, words, and service.

The faqīr humbly asks every reader who benefits from this work to remember in their blessed duʿās his noble shaykh and guide to goodness, Shaykh al-Ḥadīth Abū al-Fatḥ Muḥammad Naṣrullāh Khān al-Qādirī, his family past and future, and all those who showed him guidance, mercy, and love along the path.

May Allah accept this work with divine acceptance, place light within it, and make it a source of continuous ṣadaqah jāriyah for all who took part in its creation and transmission. May its reward flow to them in life, in the grave, and in the Hereafter as nearness to Him and to His Beloved ﷺ.

Āmīn.

بشائر الخيرات وبلوغ المسرات

THE PRAYER *of* JOYOUS TIDINGS

The Ṣalawāt of Shaykh ʿAbd al-Qādir al-Jīlānī

Translated by

DANI BIN ABDUL RAHIM

THE PRAYER OF JOYOUS TIDINGS

ISBN: 978-1-966329-70-1
979-8-295460-09-8 (INTERNATIONAL)
FIRST EDITION | DECEMBER 2025

Author:
ʿABD AL-QĀDIR AL-JĪLĀNĪ

Translator:
DANI BIN ABDUL RAHIM

Publishing Team:
SYAHIDAH AMIN (PUBLISHING COORDINATOR)
NURAISYAH RAZALI (EDITORIAL & PRODUCTION ASSOCIATE)
NURHANI IZZATI NAJIB (EDITORIAL & PRODUCTION ASSOCIATE)
ISKANDAR DZULKARNAIN (COVER DESIGNER)
NIK IRFAN HAQIMI (INTERN WINTER 2025)
AYMAN HANIFF AZLAN (OPERATIONS & PRINTING)
WAQAR ASIM (ARABIC LANGUAGE COORDINATOR)
MUHAMMAD ADNAAN SATTAUR

Imam Ghazali PUBLISHING

CONTENTS

DEDICATED IN THE MOST BLESSED & HONORING NAME OF SAYYIDUNA MUHAMMAD ﷺ and the *Ahl al-Bayt*—from the many members of the IGP community globally. A humble gift that does not honour the beloved ﷺ—rather, it honours us. The Messenger ﷺ said, "The most grateful of people to Allah are those who are most grateful to people." In honour of the

For the Beloved of Allah ﷻ from the Many Members of the IGP Community

1. Lovers of al-Habib ﷺ
2. The Ummah, past & present
3. The People of Gaza
4. The Children of Gaza
5. The People of Sudan
6. The People of Burma
7. The People of Syria
8. The People of Yemen
9. The People of Somalia
10. The Muslims of Guyana
11. The Muslims of Trinidad
12. The People of South America for their Hidaya
13. The Martyr, Sayfollah Musallet
14. Imam al-Nawawi
15. Habib Umar bin Hafiz
16. Imam al-Suyuti
17. Imam al-Sha'rani
18. Imam Ibn Abi Jamrah
19. Imam Bukhari
20. Imam Tirmidhi
21. Imam Busiri
22. Imam Sha'rawy
23. Imam al-Ghazali
24. Dawud Walid
25. Hamzah Abdul-Malik
26. Shaykh Ahmad ibn Lutfullah
27. Imam al-Bajuri
28. Imam Haddad
29. Shaykh Dr. Thaika Shu'aib
30. Sidi Ahmad Zaruq
31. Abd al-Rahman Sha'ar
32. Shaykh Salih al-Ja'fari
33. Imam al-Zarnuji
34. Qadi 'Iyad
35. Ibn Arabi
36. Ibn Kathir
37. Imam al-Shurunbulali
38. Sayyid Muhammad Alawi al-Maliki
39. Shaykh Yusuf Nabahani
40. Shaykh Abdullah Siraj al-Din
41. Ibn Rajab
42. Furhan Zubairi
43. Fatih & Yildirim
44. Husna (Umm Faris)
45. Abu Faris
46. The Muslims of New York
47. The Muslims of Malaysia
48. The Muslims of Singapore
49. The Muslims of Wisconsin
50. The Friends of Allah
51. Maulana Jalal al-Din Rumi
52. Abdallah Rothman & Family
53. Abdul Ali & Khadiza Khatun
54. Abdul Ghafoor Qureshi & Hafiza Begum
55. Abdul Khaliq Rahman & Family
56. Abdul Malik Abdul Manaf
57. Abdul Mothaher & Family
58. Abdul Razack
59. The AbdulCader Family
60. Abdullah & Fatima Kamal
61. Abdullah Gallant
62. Abida Mustafa Aura
63. Abida Sultana Chowdhry
64. Achmad Bastaman & Family
65. Adisu Jembrie & Family
66. Afaq Ahmed Khan & Gul-e-Rana
67. Ahmad El-Bkaily & Saadeen Majbour
68. Ahmed Habib & Family
69. The Ahmed Khamissa Family
70. Ahmed Saif
71. Aisha Mahdi
72. Akhtar & Khan Family & the Ummah of al-Habib ﷺ
73. Akhtar Mullick, Shamim Malik, & the Malik Family
74. Al-Hajj Qari Mohammed Ismail Yusuf Khandia
75. Al-Qulub Trust
76. Alexander Litvinenko
77. Ali Muhammad Al Momani Al Junaydi
78. Almarhum Ajum Bin Ahmad Piperdy
79. Almarhumah Jamelah Binte Abdulazis
80. Almas & Rashid Pathan
81. Alrawi & Ouklah Family
82. Amena Unnisa Khan
83. Amina Alam
84. Aminah Mahdi
85. Anissa Vakanas & Family
86. Araf Hossain
87. Armenta, Yusuf, & Femije
88. Arooz Mohammed Khan
89. Arsalan Javed & Family
90. The Arshad Butt Family
91. Arzina Ali
92. Asad & Kausar Omar
93. Asif Hussain & Family
94. Asiya Rabby
95. Asrar & Sarah
96. Ata e Ahlebaith
97. Ayaan, Alina, & Sophia with Love from Ms. Kiashe
98. Ayesha Cheema & Family
99. Ayesha Cheema & Family
100. Aysenur Ezgi Eygi
101. Aysha Akbar & Family
102. Ayub & Anees Ansari
103. Ayyub Sharif Al-Qadri
104. Bahiya Norris & Family
105. Bibi Fatma Ollite
106. Bibi Sulman Peermamode
107. Bilquis Akhtar, Mohammad Saeed & Umm Kaazim
108. Ch Karam Ellahi & Aziza Bi (Behji)
109. Daniel Omar Akhoun
110. Danish & Humaira Ahmed & Family
111. Darul Qasim College
112. Dawood Abdul Nur
113. Dhanish Mahmood & Family
114. Dirk-Uthman Hillen & Family
115. Djoewaida Gaffar & Hazaratali Dahoe
116. Dr. Yakoob Ahmed
117. Dr. Sharifah Judith Keith & Family
118. Dr. Syed Abdul Khader
119. Dunia Ali Al Momani (Umm Ahmad)
120. Eesa Hussain & Family

1500th anniversary of the Prophet's birth (The *Mawlid*), we, the wider reading community of Imam Ghazali Publishing, dedicate this work of Sayyid Shaykh ʿAbd al-Qādir al-Jīlānī as a gesture of love from him and those mentioned here. Through such inheritance, may endless divine outpourings circulate between this and the heavenly realms. *al-Fatihah.*

121. Ejaz Ahmed & Farhat Ejaz
122. Elias Varachia & Family
123. Erva Aysima & Mehmed Isa Daniyal Köse
124. Fahiem Ahmed
125. The Family of Baharin Salleh & Ruby Husain
126. The Family of Mark Crain & Hazel Gomez
127. Farhana Buccas & Farouk Khan Family
128. Farooq Family
129. Fatima Kanjo, Yusra Ayroud, Mohammed Saleem Almoshelli, Abeir Heib
130. Fatimah Zahra Khan
131. Fazilat Begum
132. Ferzanah Salim
133. Firasat Ghori & Shaykh Muhammad al-Jilani
134. Fuad Omar
135. GH, MK, M Sheik, & FZ Khan
136. Ghulam Sakina
137. GMV Family
138. Haafid, Farisa, Hasnah, & Esaam Rahman
139. Haashim Muhammad
140. Habeebunnisa
141. Habib Ahmad Mashhur al-Haddad
142. Habib Nuh Bin Muhammad Bin Zain Al-Habshi
143. Habib ur-Rehman & Imtiaz Begum
144. Habibah Chbib & Family
145. Haji Abdul Moklis
146. Haji Hassan Bin Omar & Hajjah Normah Binti Mat Said
147. Haji Mohamed Sulor bin Mohd Noor & Hajjah Rabiah binte Abdul Rahman
148. Hajjah Kousar Imtiaz
149. Hajji Muneer Ahmad Qadri
150. Halima Kamal (Leicester, UK)
151. Halimah
152. Halimah Binte Ali & Abdul Aziz Bin Rais
153. Halimah Hidayat Khan
154. Hamadi Rakdani & Mobaraka Derram
155. Hameeda Bano & Abdul-Rehman Family
156. Hameeda Mustafa Al Momani (Umm Muhammad)
157. Hamza M. Furmli
158. Hani Najib & Family
159. Hasan Bin Hinton Family
160. Haseeb & Hannah Mohammed & Family
161. Hashim & Rizwana Darbar
162. Hassan Ouklah & Family
163. Hoeseni Moharmani & Bakridi Nasroe
164. Idrees Ghusein & Family
165. Iffat Jilani
166. Ihsan & Jawaria Qureshey
167. Ihsan Yasmien Roshen
168. Ila Nur al-Ahmadi Wa al-Muhammadi Wa Ahl al-Faqrihi
169. Imambi & Abdul Majeed Desai
170. Iman S. Shahab
171. Inayat Begum
172. Inayetullah Taher
173. Insha Rabi Khaliq & Family
174. Irshad Begum & Iqbal Mirza
175. Isa Ahmad & Family
176. The Isa Family
177. Ismail & Tamachi Family
178. Ismail Family
179. Ismail Zakri bin Mohd Khalid
180. Ismatullah RA, Sharifa, Abdul Hai RA, Noah, Yusuf, & Dean Aleaf
181. Jaleeluddin Ahmed
182. Jamar bte Jamal & Abdul Rahim bin Lagiman
183. Jamil, Asha, Sajid, Zahid, & Azara Sayyidi
184. Jamshed Ahmed & the Grandparents of Faraz Hussain
185. Jawairriya Abdallah-Shahid
186. Kazi, Ukaye, Sarwa,r & Mir Family
187. Khadija & Afzaal Mohammed
188. Khadija Mahaboeb
189. Khadijah Unnisa Khan
190. Khadijah Zahra & Siddique Family
191. Khalid & Family
192. Khalid Family
193. Khalid Hussain & Family
194. Khan Muhammad Afzal
195. Late Mohammed Asif Minhas
196. Late Mubarak Ali Mohmed Bhobha
197. Leo & Luca McGlew
198. Luckun Nausheen Bibi
199. M.E.H. Khilji & Bilquis Akhter
200. Madia & Barkat Bibi
201. Al-Marhum Mahboob Mohammad Khan
202. The Family of Mahmoud Ali Fazil
203. The Family of Mohammed Moizuddin Shaikh
204. Majed & Hannah Rammouni
205. The Family Past & Present of Makhdoom Ashraf Semnani
206. Malik Fateh Khan Tiwana
207. The Manawy & al-Jamal Families
208. Marhuma Khadija Vally & Rumi Krueger & Family
209. Marhumah Zubeda Desai
210. Maria Bhatti & Family
211. Mariam Anjum & Family
212. Mariam Nazir
213. Mariam Qari-Kasim
214. Marie Hildebrandt (Umm Ahmed)
215. Masaud Parwani & Family
216. Mashooq & Waheeda Ahmed
217. Masjid Noorul Haram, Oakville Canada
218. Masood & Abdelhady Family

219. Masuma Shaban Hussain & Family
220. Mawlana Abdul Ghafoor
221. Mawlana Safiullah
222. Mawlana Waliul Hamid Aziz
223. Mehmet Ali, Selime Şahin, & Their Family Past & Future
224. Michelle Kassem & Family
225. Mohamed Hasham Varwani & Family
226. Mohamed-Fouzi Raheb & Kenza Dekar
227. Mohammad Naushad
228. Mohammad Talha Shaeque, & His Predecessors & Descendants
229. Mohammed Amin & Family (Huddersfield)
230. Mohammed Aslam
231. Mohammed Javed
232. Mohammed Junaid Ismail
233. Mohammed Khan
234. Mohammed Muhibul Islam & Family
235. Mohammed Rafiq & Family
236. Mohammed Salim & Family
237. Mohammed Shafi Lokhandwala Family
238. Mohammed Siddiq & Family
239. Moidin Palimar Family & Hammabba Adyar Family
240. Mona & Zara Ahmed
241. Mufti Omar Idris, Adib Oumer, & Family
242. Muhammad Fairuz & Family
243. Muhammad Farid Imansyah
244. Muhammad Hashim Akhtar
245. Muhammad Iskandar Dzulkarnain & Family
246. Muhammad Marzuq Shafiq
247. Muhammad Sadaq & Fatima Bi
248. Muhammad Shahabuddin
249. Muhammad Talha Ziaee
250. Muhammad Umar & Sofia Zaynab
251. Muhammad Umer & Mariam Khatri & Parents
252. Muhammad Usman Noori & Family
253. Muhammad Wasim Siddiqui & Kaniz Fatima
254. Mumtaz & Juvaria Shamsuddin
255. Murshid Ainul Huda & Family, Mureedin & Rajabalee Family
256. Muslim Ummah
257. Mustak & Zebunnisha Bukhari
258. My Beloved Mother from an Anonymous Son & Shaykh Abdul Qadir Gilani of London
259. My Beloved Murshid Shah Ahmad Noorani Siddiqui
260. Nabiel & Naael Hussain
261. Nafeesa Anjum Shaukath
262. Nasim Ahmed, Syeda Shahnaz Akhtar & Family
263. Nasreen Akhtar, Rotherham
264. Nasreen Beg & Family
265. Naveed & Al-Marhoom Ilyas Ali
266. Nazar Muhammad Qureshi & Anwar Jehan
267. Nik Irfan Haqimi
268. Noor Jahan & Mohiuddin Shaikh
269. Noor Muhammad Balouch Lashari
270. Noormahomed (Gorah) Alladee
271. Norliana Rosni
272. Nuraisyah & Family
273. Omar Obeidat
274. Osman Erbil
275. Owais Ahmed Dagra
276. The Öz Family of Chicago
277. The Parents of Shenaz & Muzaffer Satvilker
278. Parida Binte Hussain & Al-Marhumah Mariam Binte Abdullah
279. The Late Parveen Akhtar Naseem
280. Pirzada Imdad Hussain Sahib
281. R.A. & the Awliya of Allah
282. Qosia Bano
283. Rahiel Kasim
284. Raja Abgar & Musa Gerner
285. Rando Ammeralie Dahoe
286. Raphnash Raphique & Family
287. Rashid, Gul Syed, & Family
288. Saba & Maryam
289. Sabeena Munir & Junichi Jamal Watanabe
290. Sadia Shakir & Family
291. Safia & Sakhawat Hussain
292. Safiyah Hashim & Family
293. Saika Riaz
294. Sakila Binte Jalil
295. Sandra Davis & Family
296. Sarah Akhtar & Family
297. Sarah Anuar & Family
298. Sarakar Shah-e-Mira & all of his relatives
299. Sarina Rehman, Sybela Rehman, & Olga Poveteva Rehman
300. Sarosh Anwar & Janjua Family
301. Sayeeda & Saleem Ahmed
302. Sayyida Fawziyah Ebid
303. Sayyidah Hajjah Zakiya & Her Noble Family
304. Sayyidah Khadijah al-Kubra & Her Noble Family
305. Shaykh Muhamed Hydara Al-Jilani
306. Sehz M & Family
307. Seid Nasrulla Qadri Qadeeri & Family
308. Shaykh Muhamed-Sherifu's Family
309. Shabnam Sarfaraz Ahmad
310. Shahbaz Abdulkhaliq & Family
311. Shaheda Alam
312. The Shakir Family
313. Shameem Akhtar
314. Sharifah Jainah Syed Abu Bakar Barakbah & Rose Rusdi
315. Shayaan & Family
316. Shaykh Ahmad ibn Mustafa al-Alawi & All of His Relatives
317. Shaykh Hamzah wald Maqbul
318. Shaykh Hashim Al-Gailani & The Shadman Family
319. Shaykh Hassanein Muhammad Makhluf & Family
320. Shaykh Ahmed Mawlood al-Madani
321. Shaykh Ibrahim al-Yaqoubi & His Noble Family
322. Ruben Bautista & Family

323. Shaykh Ibrahim bin Ali al-Habshi & His Noble Family
324. Shaykh Imam Khaja Nasrulla
325. Shaykh Mohamed Saïdi
326. Shaykh Mohammed Amin Kholwadia, Founder & President of Darul Qasim
327. Shaykh Mokhtar Maghraoui, Ustadh Moutasem Atiya, & Their Families
328. Shaykh Muhammad Haydara al-Jilani
329. Shaykh Muhammad ibn al-Habib & His Noble Family
330. Shaykh Muhammad Adnan Darwish
331. Shaykh Musa Sugapong
332. Shaykh Mustafa Ahmad Baba & Family
333. Oscar Peña & Family
334. Shaykh Abul Huda Al-Yaqubi & Family
335. Shaykh Qadeer Pia
336. Sheikh Babikir Sheikh Nooruddin Ahmed Family & the Entire Ummah
337. Siddiqui, Khan, & Ozair Families
338. Sidi Ali al-Tamasini & All His Family
339. Sikandar Khan Sirdesai
340. Siraj al-Din 'Umar ibn 'Ali al-Zayla'i & Zayn al-Din Abdulrahman Zyka al-Zayla'i
341. Sofia Wardak & Children
342. Suraiya Essack-Varachia & Family
343. Susan Ali & Yusra Saleema Akhtar
344. Syed Afsar
345. Syed Ahad Zahid Shah
346. Syed Ahmed Family
347. Syed Ali Husain & Ghousia Begum
348. Syed Amir Zahid Shah
349. Syed Ansar
350. Syed Ibrahim & Asma Sartaj
351. Syed Jamalullah Qadri & Family
352. Syed Mubeen Saifullah
353. Syed Muhammad Ashraf
354. Syed Muhammad Iqbal Bukhari & Hafiza Iqbal Bukhari
355. Syed Rasool
356. Syed Salahuddin & Sheanaz Salahuddin
357. Syed Shahid Hassan & Family
358. Syed Shoaib & Nida Shah & Family
359. Syeda Ahmed Abu Bakr Hussayni
360. Syeda Fatimah Madinah Hussayni
361. Syeda Haseena Begum
362. Syeda Mumtaz
363. Syeda Nasira Sharieff
364. Syeda Noorein Inamdar
365. Syeda Noorjahan
366. Syeda Ruqqayah Abubaker
367. Syeda Uzma Quadri
368. Syeduna Fatima Umm al-Khair
369. Tasnim Rathur
370. Tausif Alam
371. Tayoob & Afroze Jahanger
372. Tazeem Akhtar
373. The Teachers of the Adam Family
374. The Abedrabbo Family
375. The Ahmad Family
376. The Ahsan Family
377. The Akuji & Ola Family
378. The Al Nazir Family
379. The Al-Malla Family
380. The Ali & Choudhury Family
381. The Ali Family
382. The Azam Family
383. The Baru Khan Family
384. The Believers
385. The Biabani Family
386. The Braun Family
387. The Bux & Sufi Family
388. The Cimenoglu Family
389. The El Houbba Family
390. The El-Alami Family
391. The Families of Shaan Majid & Zainab Sorathia
392. The Family & Mureeds of Shaykh Zuhoori Shah
393. The Family of Mohamed Jafaran Khan Mohamed Jalaludeen
394. The Family of Muhammad Saleem Bajwa & Kaneez Fatima
395. The Fazal-Daad Family
396. The Feyaz Ahmed Family
397. The Huseini Family
398. The Hussain Family
399. The Hussainy Family
400. The Imam Deen Family
401. The Javed Family
402. The Khan Family
403. The Lari Family
404. The Meherban Family
405. The Moosa Family
406. The Munir Family
407. The Muqeet Family
408. The Noble Souls of Tariqah Qadiriyah, Naqshbandiyah, & All
409. The Park Imtiaz Family
410. The Prophet ﷺ & the Sajjad Family
411. The Quareshy Family
412. The Rafiq Family
413. The Rasul Family
414. The Sohel, Khan, Wahdan Family
415. The Syed Saghir Hussain Shah Family
416. The Uddin Family
417. The Yasin Family, Arslan & Zainab
418. Umm Khadijah & Family
419. Usman Afzal & Family
420. Ustadha Dunia Shuaib
421. Yafees, Sharmina, Ali, Hasan, & Family
422. Yunus & Hafiza Gaibi
423. Yusuf Malik & Family
424. Zaheer Hussain & Family
425. Zahid & Shahnaz Shah & Family
426. Zahrunnissa
427. Zaib Unisa Taher
428. Zakariya Motara
429. Zameena Ally Pond
430. Zebun-Nisha Suleman
431. Zubaidah & Family
432. Zuleha & Family
433. The Sattaur Family
434. The Noble One in Sattaur & Ayube Family Lineage That First Converted to Islam
435. Muhammad al-Fatih
436. Sulaiman al-Qanuni
437. *And* ALL WHO INTENDED BUT WERE UNABLE, OR PREFERRED TO REMAIN ANONYMOUS

Publisher's Message

In the Name of Allah, Most Merciful, Most Compassionate.

Prayers of mercy and peace be upon the Master of all creation, and upon his family and companions forevermore.

Throughout the history of Islam, believers have held close a wide range of devotional litanies that nourish the heart and steady the soul. These collections of prayer, invocation, and remembrance, often called *awrād* , were preserved by scholars and saints who taught that structured remembrance strengthens a person's spiritual footing. They understood that a disciplined devotional life builds a lasting inner state. In this landscape of sacred litanies, few hold a place as widely loved and enduring as *Bashā'ir al-Khayrāt* (*The Prayer of Joyous Tidings*), the celebrated composition attributed to the great saint and spiritual reviver, Shaykh ʿAbd al-Qādir al-Jīlānī.

Bashā'ir al-Khayrāt is a litany anchored in deep reverence for the Prophet Muhammad ﷺ, overflowing with blessings, petitions, and expressions of reliance upon Allah. Its tone is one of hope and surrender, a turning of the heart toward divine generosity and mercy. The litany weaves together frequent forms of *ṣalawāt*, pleas for forgiveness and relief, and supplications for openings in matters of faith and worldly life. For centuries, it has served as a spiritual companion to seekers who wished to lighten their burdens, expand their provision, and walk through their struggles with the remembrance of Allah steady on their tongues. In a world filled with distraction, people continue to hold this litany the way one holds a lantern, something that gives clarity, warmth, and an inner sense of direction.

One of the reasons for the deep love Muslims have for *Bashā'ir al-Khayrāt* is its unique blend of tender spiritual aspiration and confident reliance upon Allah. The litany openly acknowledges human need. It teaches the believer to direct every concern to the One who Hears all things. It is a litany of openings, of *fatḥ*, and of divine good tidings, as its title suggests. For many, it feels like a door gently pushed open, an invitation to enter a space of mercy.

To understand how this litany reached so many corners of the Muslim world, one has to take a brief journey back to the lived world of its author, Shaykh ʿAbd al-Qādir al-Jīlānī. He was born in the region of Jīlān (also spelled Gīlān) in present-day Iran in 470 AH (1077–78 CE). From a young age, he showed remarkable spiritual sensitivity and an eagerness to seek knowledge. As a young man he travelled to Baghdād, one of the intellectual capitals of the Muslim world then. There he immersed himself in the study of Ḥanbalī jurisprudence, hadith, theology, and the sciences of the heart. He distinguished himself through both mastery of the outward religious disciplines and a deep inner humility that endeared him to scholars and common people alike.

Shaykh ʿAbd al-Qādir al-Jīlānī soon became recognised as a scholar whose presence elevated hearts. His sermons were known for moving even the most hardened individuals to repentance and sincerity. He became a point of mercy for people overwhelmed by their struggles, offering spiritual guidance that was both grounded and filled with compassion. As his influence grew, students gathered around him. Jurists, ascetics, merchants, and ordinary believers sought from him both religious instruction and spiritual refinement. His reputation as *Sulṭān al-Awliyāʾ*, the "Leader of the Saints," emerged from a lifetime spent guiding people to turn back to God with honesty and devotion.

It was in this environment of teaching, worship, and service that many of his litanies, discourses, and supplications were preserved, including *Bashāʾir al-Khayrāt*. His students carefully transmitted his words, memorising and recording them, and carrying them far beyond Baghdād. Though he was primarily a jurist and theologian by training, his spiritual teachings shaped the foundations of what would later become the Qādirī order, one of the most widespread and enduring spiritual paths in the Muslim world. His message resonated because it combined clarity of doctrine with gentleness of heart. He reminded people that the door of Divine Mercy is wide, and that the most honoured before God are those whose hearts remain soft.

After Shaykh ʿAbd al-Qādir's passing in 561 AH (1166 CE), his students and their successors continued to teach his devotional traditions. Baghdād remained a beacon of learning, and pilgrims travelling for Hajj or seeking knowledge often carried his teachings with them as they moved across regions. Over the next centuries, the Qādirī path spread across Iraq, Syria, Egypt, the Ḥijāz, and deeply into North Africa. By the 7th and 8th centuries AH, Qādirī lodges and Zawāyā had become established in cities such as Damascus, Cairo, Tunis, Fez, and Alexandria. Teachers in these regions included *Bashāʾir al-Khayrāt* within their daily litanies, teaching it to students and communities who found comfort and beauty in its words.

The spread extended far beyond the Arab world. As trade routes and scholarly networks expanded, Qādirī scholars travelled into Anatolia, the Balkans, Persia, East Africa, and the Indian subcontinent. In each of these regions, *Bashāʾir al-Khayrāt* found a new home. Families in Sudan and Somalia recited it on Fridays. Scholars in India included it in their devotional manuals. East African communities recited it in gatherings of remembrance. In Southeast Asia, particularly Indonesia and Malaysia, the Qādirī path became woven into the devotional fabric of the region, and the litany was embraced by spiritual teachers who recognised its uplifting nature.

The litany spread so widely because of its spiritual texture. It speaks to a timeless human longing, the desire for relief, clarity, forgiveness, and nearness to Divine Mercy. It offers a language for the heart, one that is simple enough for the ordinary believer and profound enough for the most learned scholar. Its frequent focus on sending blessings upon the Prophet Muhammad ﷺ reflects a core truth of Islamic spirituality, *ṣalawāt* is a doorway through which Divine Lights enter the believer's life. The Qurʾan itself commands believers to send blessings upon the Prophet, and countless aḥādīth describe the transformative effects of doing so. Shaykh ʿAbd al-Qādir al-Jīlānī understood this deeply, and *Bashāʾir al-Khayrāt* reflects that understanding with serenity and confidence.

Sending blessings upon the Prophet ﷺ is an act of love and an act of self-purification. It polishes the heart, increases one's spiritual focus, and draws a person closer to the Prophetic character. The litany emphasises these blessings repeatedly, reminding the reader that the Prophet ﷺ is a mercy for all worlds, and that aligning oneself with him brings tremendous spiritual benefit. Embedded within its lines are Qurʾanic references, *duʿāʾ* for forgiveness, and appeals for divine openings. These layers invite the believer to approach the litany with sincerity, attentiveness, and hope.

Equally important is the litany's emphasis on seeking Divine Protection and Aid. It acknowledges the reality of difficulty, grief, and constriction. *Bashā'ir al-Khayrāt* teaches that faith transforms hardship. It encourages the believer to hand over their anxieties to Allah, trusting that what He decrees is ultimately for their benefit. The supplications included in the litany encompass both this world and the next, asking Allah to illuminate the believer's heart, ease their path, forgive their shortcomings, and bring them into His Mercy in this life and the Hereafter. These are universal concerns. People today carry the same worries people carried centuries ago. For this reason, the litany remains as relevant now as it was when it first spread from Baghdād.

In many regions, *Bashā'ir al-Khayrāt* became a communal practice. It was recited in groups after Jumuʿah, in gatherings of remembrance, and in moments of communal need. People recite it when seeking Divine Openings for marriage, livelihood, health, safety, or major decisions. It became one of the spiritual anchors of Qādirī devotional life. Its reach expanded far beyond formal Sufi settings. Many Muslims who did not identify with any particular spiritual order still adopted the litany simply because of its beauty and emotional power. It became, in a sense, a shared inheritance.

Today, in an age of unprecedented distraction and inner restlessness, the wisdom of structured devotion feels more vital than ever. People are searching for practices that bring calm, grounding, and genuine nearness to Allah. *Bashā'ir al-Khayrāt* offers exactly that. It is a litany that slows down the racing mind. It asks the believer to pause, breathe, and remember. It returns one to the essentials, gratitude, repentance, hope, and love of the Prophet ﷺ. If approached with sincerity, it becomes a relationship, a quiet companionship that steadies the heart throughout the day.

Reciting this litany places the believer in a long, unbroken chain of hearts. Men and women, scholars and merchants, students and elders turned to these same words seeking mercy. The fact that it has survived across centuries, continents, cultures, and languages is itself a testament to its spiritual depth. It continues to soften hearts in Sudan, resonate in mosques in India, be taught in gatherings in Indonesia, and be cherished in homes across the Muslim world. The believer who recites it today joins a global community bound together by devotion.

As you read this litany, approach it gently. Let each blessing upon the Prophet ﷺ settle in your chest. Allow the supplications to remind you of Allah's Generosity. Bring your needs, your concerns, and your hopes into the recitation. God's Mercy is vast, and these words have carried the prayers of countless people before you. May Allah make this litany a source of light for you, a means of forgiveness, and a path to the openings you seek. May He place tranquility in your heart, clarity in your affairs, and blessing in your days. And may the prayers you recite upon His beloved Prophet ﷺ become a source of nearness to Him in this world and the next.

Author's Introduction

In the Name of Allah, Most Merciful, Most Compassionate.

Prayers of mercy and peace be upon the Master of all creation, and upon his family and companions forevermore.

THE PRAYER OF JOYOUS TIDINGS OF GOODNESS UPON OUR MASTER, THE PROPHET ﷺ

Attributed to the shaykh of the ummah, the foremost of the imams, the master of the nobles, the paramount spiritual axis, the supreme succour, the most generous refuge, my master ʿAbd al-Qādir al-Jīlānī (may Allah sanctify his secret and benefit us through him). He said to some of his brethren, whom he loved purely for Allah's sake, "Take these prayers from me, for I received them by inspiration from Allah Almighty, then I presented them to the Prophet ﷺ."

In the Name of Allah, Most Merciful, Most Compassionate.

"Indeed, Allah showers His blessings upon the Prophet, and His angels pray for him. O believers! Invoke Allah's blessings upon him and salute him with worthy greetings of peace."

JOYOUS TIDINGS OF GOODNESS

In the Name of Allah, Most Merciful, Most Compassionate. All praise belongs to Allah alone, who has graced us with faith. Prayers of mercy and peace be upon the Master of all creation, and upon his family and companions forevermore.

To commence. It has been narrated that the shaykh of the ummah, the foremost of the imams, the master of the nobles, the paramount spiritual axis, the supreme succour, the most generous refuge, my master ʿAbd al-Qādir al-Jīlānī, said to some of his brethren, whom he loved purely for Allah's sake, "Take these prayers from me, for I received them by inspiration from Allah Almighty, then I presented them to the Prophet ﷺ. I wished to ask him about their merit, but before I could..." [he said to me]:

> "They hold a tremendous merit beyond measure: they lift those who recite them to the loftiest degrees and lead them to the ultimate ends. Whoever seeks a need through them will not return disappointed, nor will his hope be in vain, nor his supplication rejected. And whoever recites them, even once, or carries them with him, Allah will forgive him and those present in his company. When his appointed time of death arrives, four of the angels of mercy will be with him: The first will shield him from Satan; the second will inspire him with the testimony of faith; the third will offer him to drink from al-Kawthar; and the fourth, bearing in his hand a golden vessel filled with the fruits of Paradise, will bring him glad tidings of his dwelling therein, saying: 'Rejoice, O servant of Allah!' Then he will behold it with his own eyes before his soul departs, and he will enter his grave safe, joyful, and content, finding neither loneliness nor constriction therein. Forty gates of mercy will be opened for him, together with forty gates of light.
>
> He will be resurrected on the Day of Judgement, and there will be an angel on his right giving him joyous tidings, and another on his left assuring him of safety. Arrayed in two robes of honour, he will be given a noble steed to mount; he shall know neither grief nor remorse, and his account will be light.
>
> As he crosses the Bridge, the Fire will cry out: 'Hurry across, O servant freed by Allah! I am forbidden to you.'
>
> He will enter Paradise among the forerunners. There he shall be granted forty domes of radiant white silver; within each dome, a palace of gold; within each palace, a hundred pavilions of light. In every pavilion is a couch of green silk, and upon each couch rests a maiden of

> wide-eyed beauty, fashioned from the purest fragrance, like the full moon at the height of its splendour. Then he will be granted what no eye has ever seen, no ear has ever heard, and what has never crossed the heart of man."

It is reported that on the night of the Prophet's ﷺ Ascent to his Lord, the Almighty said to him:

> "Who does the earth belong to, O Muhammad?"
> He replied, "To You, my Lord."
> "And who do the heavens belong to, O Muhammad?"
> He replied, "To You, my Lord."
> "And who do the veils belong to, O Muhammad?"
> He replied, "To You, my Lord."
> "And who does the Throne belong to, O Muhammad?"
> He replied, "To You, my Lord."
> "And who do you belong to, O Muhammad?"

At this, the Prophet ﷺ fell in prostration, his modesty holding him back from responding. Then the Almighty said, "You belong to the one who prays for blessings upon you." Thereby was he raised in honour and exaltation. My master ʿAbd al-Qādir al-Jīlānī said:

> "This is the prayer most fitting for this narration. It opens seventy gates of mercy, unveils wonders along the path to Paradise, and surpasses the freeing of a thousand souls, the sacrifice of a thousand camels, the giving of a thousand dinars in charity, and the fasting of a thousand months. Within it lies a hidden secret. Through it, provision is made easy, character traits are refined, needs are met, ranks are raised, sins are erased, faults are veiled, and the lowly are raised in honour."

My master Makīn al-Dīn said:

> "This prayer is bestowed only upon a righteous and perfected man. It is perfect in its qualities, encompassing every bounty. When one who holds to it is troubled by some affair, every one of its prayers becomes a means

for him with the noble Prophet ﷺ, and every one of its verses becomes an intercessor for him with the Lord Almighty. It is the prayer of those who pray, the recital of those who remember, the admonition of those who take heed, the means of those who entreat, and it is the prayer of the Glorious Qur'an. I have named it *Joyous Tidings of Goodness (Bashā'ir al-Khayrāt).* And lo, here is that very prayer."

بشائر الخيرات وبلوغ المسرات

THE PRAYER *of* JOYOUS TIDINGS

The Ṣalawāt of Shaykh ʿAbd al-Qādir al-Jīlānī

Translated by

DANI BIN ABDUL RAHIM

أعوذ بالله من الشيطان الرجيم

I seek refuge with Allah from the accursed Satan

بسم الله الرحمن الرحيم

In the Name of Allah Most Merciful Most Compassionate.

إن الله وملائكته يصلون على النبي يا أيها الذين آمنوا صلوا عليه وسلموا تسليما

Verily, Allah and His Angels send prayers upon the Prophet;
O you who believe, send prayers and peace upon him

PRAYER ONE

اللَّهُمَّ صَلِّ وَسَلِّمْ عَلَى سَيِّدِنَا مُحَمَّدٍ الْبَشِيرِ الْمُبَشِّرِ لِلْمُؤْمِنِينَ بِمَا قَالَ اللهُ الْعَظِيم
﴿وَبَشِّرِ ٱلْمُؤْمِنِينَ ۝٨٧﴾ ﴿وَأَنَّ ٱللَّهَ لَا يُضِيعُ أَجْرَ ٱلْمُؤْمِنِينَ ۝١٧١﴾.

O Allah, send mercy and peace upon our master Muhammad, the bearer of good news, who conveys Your joyous tidings to the believers: "And give good news to the believers;"[1] "Allah does not deny the reward of the believers."[2]

1 *Yūnus*, 87.

2 *Āl ʿImrān*, 171.

PRAYER TWO

اللَّهُمَّ صَلِّ وَسَلِّمْ عَلَى سَيِّدِنَا مُحَمَّدٍ الْبَشِيرِ الْمُبَشِّرِ لِلذَّاكِرِينَ بِمَا قَالَ اللهُ الْعَظِيم
﴿فَاذْكُرُونِيٓ أَذْكُرْكُمْ ١٥٢﴾ ﴿ٱذْكُرُواْ ٱللَّهَ ذِكْرًا كَثِيرًا ٤١ وَسَبِّحُوهُ
بُكْرَةً وَأَصِيلًا ٤٢ هُوَ ٱلَّذِى يُصَلِّى عَلَيْكُمْ وَمَلَٰٓئِكَتُهُۥ لِيُخْرِجَكُم
مِّنَ ٱلظُّلُمَٰتِ إِلَى ٱلنُّورِ ۚ وَكَانَ بِٱلْمُؤْمِنِينَ رَحِيمًا ٤٣ تَحِيَّتُهُمْ يَوْمَ
يَلْقَوْنَهُۥ سَلَٰمٌ ۚ وَأَعَدَّ لَهُمْ أَجْرًا كَرِيمًا ٤٤﴾.

O Allah, send mercy and peace upon our master Muhammad, the bearer of good news, who conveys Your joyous tidings to those devoted to Your remembrance: "Remember Me; I will remember you;"[3] "always remember Allah often, and glorify Him morning and evening. He is the One Who showers His blessings upon you – and His angels pray for you – so that He may bring you out of darkness and into light. For He is ever Merciful to the believers. Their greeting on the Day they meet Him will be, 'Peace!' And He has prepared for them an honourable reward."[4]

3 *Al-Baqarah*, 152.

4 *Al-Aḥzāb*, 41–44. Some manuscripts do not include verse 44, however, we have chosen to include it.

PRAYER THREE

اللَّهُمَّ صَلِّ وَسَلِّمْ عَلَى سَيِّدِنَا مُحَمَّدٍ الْبَشِيرِ الْمُبَشِّرِ لِلْعَامِلِينَ بِمَا قَالَ اللهُ الْعَظِيم
﴿أَنِّي لَآ أُضِيعُ عَمَلَ عَٰمِلٖ مِّنكُم مِّن ذَكَرٍ أَوۡ أُنثَىٰۖ ١٩٥﴾ ﴿وَمَنۡ
عَمِلَ صَٰلِحٗا مِّن ذَكَرٍ أَوۡ أُنثَىٰ وَهُوَ مُؤۡمِنٞ فَأُوْلَٰٓئِكَ يَدۡخُلُونَ ٱلۡجَنَّةَ
يُرۡزَقُونَ فِيهَا بِغَيۡرِ حِسَابٖ ٤٠﴾.

O Allah, send mercy and peace upon our master Muhammad, the bearer of good news, who conveys Your joyous tidings to those who act righteously: "I will never deny any of you – male or female – the reward of your deeds;"[5] "whoever does an evil deed will only be paid back with its equivalent. And whoever does good, whether male or female, and is a believer, they will enter Paradise, where they will be provided for without limit."[6]

5 *Āl ʿImrān*, 195.
6 *Ghāfir*, 40.

PRAYER FOUR

اللَّهُمَّ صَلِّ وَسَلِّمْ عَلَى سَيِّدِنَا مُحَمَّدٍ الْبَشِيرِ الْمُبَشِّرِ لِلْأَوَّابِينَ بِمَا قَالَ اللهُ الْعَظِيم
﴿فَإِنَّهُۥ كَانَ لِلْأَوَّٰبِينَ غَفُورًا ٢٥﴾ ﴿لَهُم مَّا يَشَآءُونَ عِندَ رَبِّهِمْۚ ذَٰلِكَ
جَزَآءُ ٱلْمُحْسِنِينَ ٣٤﴾.

O Allah, send mercy and peace upon our master Muhammad, the bearer of good news, who conveys Your joyous tidings to those who ever turn back in repentance: "He is certainly All-Forgiving to those who constantly turn to Him;"[7] "they will have whatever they desire with their Lord. That is the reward of those who do good."[8]

7 *Al-Isrā'*, 25.

8 *Al-Zumar*, 34.

PRAYER FIVE

اللَّهُمَّ صَلِّ وَسَلِّمْ عَلَى سَيِّدِنَا مُحَمَّدٍ الْبَشِيرِ الْمُبَشِّرِ لِلتَّوَّابِينَ بِمَا قَالَ اللهُ الْعَظِيم
﴿إِنَّ ٱللَّهَ يُحِبُّ ٱلتَّوَّٰبِينَ وَيُحِبُّ ٱلْمُتَطَهِّرِينَ ٢٢٢﴾ ﴿وَهُوَ ٱلَّذِى يَقْبَلُ
ٱلتَّوْبَةَ عَنْ عِبَادِهِۦ وَيَعْفُوا۟ عَنِ ٱلسَّيِّـَٔاتِ ٢٥﴾.

O Allah, send mercy and peace upon our master Muhammad, the bearer of good news, who conveys Your joyous tidings to those who unfailingly repent: "Surely Allah loves those who always turn to Him in repentance and those who purify themselves;"[9] "He is the One Who accepts repentance from His servants and pardons their sins."[10]

9 *Al-Baqarah*, 222.
10 *Al-Shūrā*, 25.

PRAYER SIX

اللَّهُمَّ صَلِّ وَسَلِّمْ عَلَى سَيِّدِنَا مُحَمَّدٍ الْبَشِيرِ الْمُبَشِّرِ لِلْمُخْلِصِينَ بِمَا قَالَ اللهُ الْعَظِيم
﴿فَمَن كَانَ يَرْجُواْ لِقَآءَ رَبِّهِۦ فَلْيَعْمَلْ عَمَلًا صَٰلِحًا وَلَا يُشْرِكْ بِعِبَادَةِ
رَبِّهِۦٓ أَحَدًۢا ﴿١١٠﴾﴾ ﴿مُخْلِصِينَ لَهُ ٱلدِّينَ ﴿٥﴾﴾.

O Allah, send mercy and peace upon our master
Muhammad, the bearer of good news, who conveys
Your joyous tidings to those devoted with pure sincerity:
"Anyone who fears to meet his Lord should do good deeds
and give no one a share in the worship due to his Lord;"[11]
"sincerely devoted to Him alone."[12]

11 *Al-Kahf*, 110.
12 *Al-Bayyinah*, 5.

PRAYER SEVEN

اللَّهُمَّ صَلِّ وَسَلِّمْ عَلَى سَيِّدِنَا مُحَمَّدٍ الْبَشِيرِ الْمُبَشِّرِ لِلْمُصَلِّينَ بِمَا قَالَ اللهُ الْعَظِيم
﴿وَأَقِمِ ٱلصَّلَوٰةَۖ إِنَّ ٱلصَّلَوٰةَ تَنْهَىٰ عَنِ ٱلْفَحْشَآءِ وَٱلْمُنكَرِۗ ٤٥﴾ ﴿أَقِمِ
ٱلصَّلَوٰةَ وَأْمُرْ بِٱلْمَعْرُوفِ وَٱنْهَ عَنِ ٱلْمُنكَرِ وَٱصْبِرْ عَلَىٰ مَآ أَصَابَكَۖ إِنَّ
ذَٰلِكَ مِنْ عَزْمِ ٱلْأُمُورِ ١٧﴾.

O Allah, send mercy and peace upon our master Muhammad, the bearer of good news, who conveys Your joyous tidings to those dedicated to prayer: "Establish the prayer. Indeed, the prayer restrains indecency and wickedness;"[13] "establish prayer, encourage what is good and forbid what is evil, and endure patiently whatever befalls you. Surely this is a resolve to aspire to."[14]

13 *Al-ʿAnkabūt*, 45.

14 *Luqmān*, 17.

PRAYER EIGHT

اللَّهُمَّ صَلِّ وَسَلِّمْ عَلَى سَيِّدِنَا مُحَمَّدٍ الْبَشِيرِ الْمُبَشِّرِ لِلْخَاشِعِينَ بِمَا قَالَ اللهُ الْعَظِيم
﴿وَٱسْتَعِينُواْ بِٱلصَّبْرِ وَٱلصَّلَوٰةِۚ وَإِنَّهَا لَكَبِيرَةٌ إِلَّا عَلَى ٱلْخَٰشِعِينَ ٤٥
ٱلَّذِينَ يَظُنُّونَ أَنَّهُم مُّلَٰقُواْ رَبِّهِمْ وَأَنَّهُمْ إِلَيْهِ رَٰجِعُونَ ٤٦﴾ ﴿ٱلَّذِينَ
يَذْكُرُونَ ٱللَّهَ قِيَٰمًا وَقُعُودًا وَعَلَىٰ جُنُوبِهِمْ وَيَتَفَكَّرُونَ فِى خَلْقِ
ٱلسَّمَٰوَٰتِ وَٱلْأَرْضِ رَبَّنَا مَا خَلَقْتَ هَٰذَا بَٰطِلًا سُبْحَٰنَكَ فَقِنَا عَذَابَ
ٱلنَّارِ ١٩١﴾.

O Allah, send mercy and peace upon our master Muhammad, the bearer of good news, who conveys Your joyous tidings to the humble: "And seek help through patience and prayer. Indeed, it is a burden except for the humble – those who are certain that they will meet their Lord and to Him they will return;"[15] "they are those who remember Allah while standing, sitting, and lying on their sides, and reflect on the creation of the heavens and the earth and pray, 'Our Lord! You have not created all of this without purpose. Glory be to You! Protect us from the torment of the Fire.'"[16]

---

15 *Al-Baqarah*, 45-46.
16 *Āl ʿImrān*, 191.

PRAYER NINE

اللَّهُمَّ صَلِّ وَسَلِّمْ عَلَى سَيِّدِنَا مُحَمَّدٍ الْبَشِيرِ الْمُبَشِّرِ لِلصَّابِرِينَ بِمَا قَالَ اللهُ الْعَظِيم ﴿إِنَّمَا يُوَفَّى ٱلصَّٰبِرُونَ أَجْرَهُم بِغَيْرِ حِسَابٖ ١٠﴾ ﴿أُوْلَٰٓئِكَ ٱلَّذِينَ هَدَىٰهُمُ ٱللَّهُۖ وَأُوْلَٰٓئِكَ هُمْ أُوْلُواْ ٱلْأَلْبَٰبِ ١٨﴾.

O Allah, send mercy and peace upon our master Muhammad, the bearer of good news, who conveys Your joyous tidings to those of unswerving patience: "Only those who endure patiently will be given their reward without limit;"[17] "these are the ones Allah has guided, and these are the people of insight."[18]

17 *Al-Zumar*, 10.
18 *Al-Zumar*, 18.

PRAYER TEN

اللَّهُمَّ صَلِّ وَسَلِّمْ عَلَى سَيِّدِنَا مُحَمَّدٍ الْبَشِيرِ الْمُبَشِّرِ لِلْخَائِفِينَ بِمَا قَالَ اللهُ الْعَظِيم
﴿وَلِمَنْ خَافَ مَقَامَ رَبِّهِۦ جَنَّتَانِ ﴿٤٦﴾﴾ ﴿وَأَمَّا مَنْ خَافَ مَقَامَ رَبِّهِۦ
وَنَهَى ٱلنَّفْسَ عَنِ ٱلْهَوَىٰ ﴿٤٠﴾ فَإِنَّ ٱلْجَنَّةَ هِىَ ٱلْمَأْوَىٰ ﴿٤١﴾﴾.

O Allah, send mercy and peace upon our master Muhammad, the bearer of good news, who conveys Your joyous tidings to those in fearful awe of You: "And whoever is in fearful awe of standing before their Lord will have two Gardens;"[19] "and as for whoever is in fearful awe of standing before their Lord and restrains himself from base desires, Paradise will certainly be his home."[20]

19 *Al-Raḥmān*, 46.
20 *Al-Nāziʿāt*, 40–41.

PRAYER ELEVEN

اللَّهُمَّ صَلِّ وَسَلِّمْ عَلَى سَيِّدِنَا مُحَمَّدٍ الْبَشِيرِ الْمُبَشِّرِ لِلْمُتَّقِينَ بِمَا قَالَ اللهُ الْعَظِيم
﴿وَرَحۡمَتِي وَسِعَتۡ كُلَّ شَيۡءٖۚ فَسَأَكۡتُبُهَا لِلَّذِينَ يَتَّقُونَ وَيُؤۡتُونَ
ٱلزَّكَوٰةَ وَٱلَّذِينَ هُم بِـَٔايَٰتِنَا يُؤۡمِنُونَ ١٥٦ ٱلَّذِينَ يَتَّبِعُونَ ٱلرَّسُولَ
ٱلنَّبِيَّ ٱلۡأُمِّيَّ ١٥٧﴾ ﴿لَهُمۡ جَزَآءُ ٱلضِّعۡفِ بِمَا عَمِلُواْ وَهُمۡ فِي ٱلۡغُرُفَٰتِ
ءَامِنُونَ ٣٧﴾.

O Allah, send mercy and peace upon our master Muhammad, the bearer of good news, who conveys Your joyous tidings to the conscientious: "But My mercy encompasses everything. I will ordain mercy for those who are conscientious, pay alms-tax, and believe in Our revelations; who follow the Messenger, the *ummī* Prophet;"[21] "they will have a multiplied reward for what they did, and they will be secure in elevated mansions."[22]

---

21 *Al-Aʿrāf*, 156–157.

22 *Saba'*, 37.

PRAYER TWELVE

اللَّهُمَّ صَلِّ وَسَلِّمْ عَلَى سَيِّدِنَا مُحَمَّدٍ الْبَشِيرِ الْمُبَشِّرِ لِلْمُخْبِتِينَ بِمَا قَالَ اللهُ الْعَظِيم
﴿وَبَشِّرِ ٱلْمُخْبِتِينَ ٣٤ ٱلَّذِينَ إِذَا ذُكِرَ ٱللَّهُ وَجِلَتْ قُلُوبُهُمْ ٣٥﴾
﴿وَٱلَّذِينَ يُؤْتُونَ مَآ ءَاتَوا۟ وَّقُلُوبُهُمْ وَجِلَةٌ أَنَّهُمْ إِلَىٰ رَبِّهِمْ رَٰجِعُونَ ٦٠
أُو۟لَـٰٓئِكَ يُسَـٰرِعُونَ فِى ٱلْخَيْرَٰتِ وَهُمْ لَهَا سَـٰبِقُونَ ٦١﴾.

O Allah, send mercy and peace upon our master Muhammad, the bearer of good news, who conveys Your joyous tidings to those who are humble with serenity: "Give good news to those of serene humility – whose hearts tremble at the remembrance of Allah;"[23] and "who always give with hearts that tremble, knowing that they will return to Him – it is they who race to do good deeds, always taking the lead."[24]

23 *Al-Ḥajj*, 34-35.

24 *Al-Mu'minūn*, 60–61. Verse 61 has been added as it is found in some manuscripts.

PRAYER THIRTEEN

اللَّهُمَّ صَلِّ وَسَلِّمْ عَلَى سَيِّدِنَا مُحَمَّدٍ الْبَشِيرِ الْمُبَشِّرِ لِلصَّابِرِينَ بِمَا قَالَ اللهُ الْعَظِيمُ
﴿وَبَشِّرِ ٱلصَّـٰبِرِينَ ١٥٥ ٱلَّذِينَ إِذَآ أَصَـٰبَتۡهُم مُّصِيبَةٌ قَالُوٓاْ إِنَّا لِلَّهِ وَإِنَّآ
إِلَيۡهِ رَٰجِعُونَ ١٥٦ أُوْلَـٰٓئِكَ عَلَيۡهِمۡ صَلَوَٰتٌ مِّن رَّبِّهِمۡ وَرَحۡمَةٌۖ وَأُوْلَـٰٓئِكَ
هُمُ ٱلۡمُهۡتَدُونَ ١٥٧﴾ ﴿إِنِّي جَزَيۡتُهُمُ ٱلۡيَوۡمَ بِمَا صَبَرُوٓاْ أَنَّهُمۡ هُمُ
ٱلۡفَآئِزُونَ ١١١﴾.

O Allah, send mercy and peace upon our master Muhammad, the bearer of good news, who conveys Your joyous tidings to those who are steadfast in patience: "Give good news to those who patiently endure – who say, when struck by a disaster, 'surely to Allah we belong and to Him we will return;' they are the ones who will receive Allah's blessings and mercy; and it is they who are rightly guided;"[25] "today I have indeed rewarded them for their patience: they are certainly the triumphant."[26]

25 *Al-Baqarah*, 155–157.
26 *Al-Mu'minūn*, 111.

PRAYER FOURTEEN

اللَّهُمَّ صَلِّ وَسَلِّمْ عَلَى سَيِّدِنَا مُحَمَّدٍ الْبَشِيرِ الْمُبَشِّرِ لِلْكَاظِمِينَ بِمَا قَالَ اللهُ
الْعَظِيمِ ﴿وَٱلْكَٰظِمِينَ ٱلْغَيْظَ وَٱلْعَافِينَ عَنِ ٱلنَّاسِۗ وَٱللَّهُ يُحِبُّ
ٱلْمُحْسِنِينَ ١٣٤﴾ ﴿فَمَنْ عَفَا وَأَصْلَحَ فَأَجْرُهُۥ عَلَى ٱللَّهِۚ إِنَّهُۥ لَا يُحِبُّ
ٱلظَّٰلِمِينَ ٤٠﴾.

O Allah, send mercy and peace upon our master Muhammad, the bearer of good news, who conveys Your joyous tidings to those who curb their inner rage: "Those who hold back their seething rage, and pardon others – Allah loves those who do good;"[27] "whoever pardons and seeks reconciliation, then their reward is with Allah. He certainly does not like who do wrong."[28]

27 *Āl ʿImrān*, 134.

28 *Al-Shūrā*, 40.

PRAYER FIFTEEN

اللَّهُمَّ صَلِّ وَسَلِّمْ عَلَى سَيِّدِنَا مُحَمَّدٍ الْبَشِيرِ الْمُبَشِّرِ لِلْمُحْسِنِينَ بِمَا قَالَ اللهُ الْعَظِيمِ
﴿وَأَحْسِنُوٓا۟ ۛ إِنَّ ٱللَّهَ يُحِبُّ ٱلْمُحْسِنِينَ ١٩٥﴾ ﴿مَن جَآءَ بِٱلْحَسَنَةِ
فَلَهُۥ عَشْرُ أَمْثَالِهَا ۖ وَمَن جَآءَ بِٱلسَّيِّئَةِ فَلَا يُجْزَىٰٓ إِلَّا مِثْلَهَا وَهُمْ لَا
يُظْلَمُونَ ١٦٠﴾.

O Allah, send mercy and peace upon our master Muhammad, the bearer of good news, who conveys Your joyous tidings to those who do good: "And do good, for Allah certainly loves those who do so;"[29] "whoever comes with a good deed will be rewarded tenfold, but whoever comes with a bad deed will be punished for only one – none will be wronged."[30]

---

29 *Al-Baqarah*, 195.

30 *Al-Anʿām*, 160.

PRAYER SIXTEEN

اللَّهُمَّ صَلِّ وَسَلِّمْ عَلَى سَيِّدِنَا مُحَمَّدٍ الْبَشِيرِ الْمُبَشِّرِ لِلْمُتَصَدِّقِينَ بِمَا قَالَ اللهُ الْعَظِيم ﴿وَأَن تَصَدَّقُواْ خَيْرٌ لَّكُمْ إِن كُنتُمْ تَعْلَمُونَ ﴿٢٨٠﴾﴾ ﴿إِنَّ ٱللَّهَ يَجْزِى ٱلْمُتَصَدِّقِينَ ﴿٨٨﴾﴾.

O Allah, send mercy and peace upon our master Muhammad, the bearer of good news, who conveys Your joyous tidings to those who are charitable: "to forgive the debt in charity is better for you, if any of you but knew;"[31] and "verily Allah magnificently repays the charitable."[32]

31 *Al-Baqarah*, 280.

32 *Yūsuf*, 88.

PRAYER SEVENTEEN

اللَّهُمَّ صَلِّ وَسَلِّمْ عَلَى سَيِّدِنَا مُحَمَّدٍ الْبَشِيرِ الْمُبَشِّرِ لِلْمُنْفِقِينَ بِمَا قَالَ اللهُ الْعَظِيم
﴿وَمِمَّا رَزَقْنَٰهُمْ يُنفِقُونَ ٣٥﴾ ﴿وَمَآ أَنفَقْتُم مِّن شَيْءٍ فَهُوَ يُخْلِفُهُۥ
وَهُوَ خَيْرُ ٱلرَّٰزِقِينَ ٣٩﴾.

O Allah, send mercy and peace upon our master Muhammad, the bearer of good news, who conveys Your joyous tidings to those who are unstintingly openhanded: "And they donate from what We have provided for them;"[33] "and whatever you spend in charity, He will compensate you for it, for He is the best of providers."[34]

33 *Al-Ḥajj*, 35.
34 *Saba'*, 39.

PRAYER EIGHTEEN

اللَّهُمَّ صَلِّ وَسَلِّمْ عَلَى سَيِّدِنَا مُحَمَّدٍ الْبَشِيرِ الْمُبَشِّرِ لِلشَّاكِرِينَ بِمَا قَالَ اللهُ الْعَظِيمُ
﴿وَٱشْكُرُواْ نِعْمَتَ ٱللَّهِ إِن كُنتُمْ إِيَّاهُ تَعْبُدُونَ ﴿١١٤﴾﴾ ﴿لَئِن شَكَرْتُمْ
لَأَزِيدَنَّكُمْ وَلَئِن كَفَرْتُمْ إِنَّ عَذَابِى لَشَدِيدٌ ﴿٧﴾﴾.

O Allah, send mercy and peace upon our master Muhammad, the bearer of good news, who conveys Your joyous tidings to the thankful: "And be grateful for the blessing of Allah, if it be Him you truly worship;"[35] "If you are grateful, I will certainly give you more. But if you are ungrateful, surely My punishment is severe."[36]

35 *Al-Naḥl,* 114.
36 *Ibrahīm,* 7.

PRAYER NINETEEN

اللَّهُمَّ صَلِّ وَسَلِّمْ عَلَى سَيِّدِنَا مُحَمَّدٍ الْبَشِيرِ الْمُبَشِّرِ لِلسَّائِلِينَ بِمَا قَالَ اللهُ الْعَظِيمِ
﴿فَإِنِّي قَرِيبٌ ۖ أُجِيبُ دَعْوَةَ ٱلدَّاعِ إِذَا دَعَانِ ۖ ﴿١٨٦﴾﴾ ﴿ٱدْعُونِىٓ أَسْتَجِبْ
لَكُمْ ۚ ﴿٦٠﴾﴾.

O Allah, send mercy and peace upon our master Muhammad, the bearer of good news, who conveys Your joyous tidings to those who implore You: "I am truly near; I respond to one's prayer when they call upon Me;"[37] "call upon Me, I will respond to you."[38]

37 *Al-Baqarah*, 186.
38 *Ghāfir*, 60.

PRAYER TWENTY

اللَّهُمَّ صَلِّ وَسَلِّمْ عَلَى سَيِّدِنَا مُحَمَّدٍ الْبَشِيرِ الْمُبَشِّرِ لِلصَّالِحِينَ بِمَا قَالَ اللهُ الْعَظِيم
﴿أَنَّ ٱلْأَرْضَ يَرِثُهَا عِبَادِيَ ٱلصَّٰلِحُونَ ۝١٠٥﴾ ﴿أُوْلَٰٓئِكَ هُمُ ٱلْوَٰرِثُونَ
۝١٠ ٱلَّذِينَ يَرِثُونَ ٱلْفِرْدَوْسَ هُمْ فِيهَا خَٰلِدُونَ ۝١١﴾.

O Allah, send mercy and peace upon our master Muhammad, the bearer of good news, who conveys Your joyous tidings to the righteous: "My righteous servants shall inherit the earth;"[39] "these are the ones who will be awarded Paradise as their own. They will be there forever."[40]

39 *Al-Anbiyā'*, 105.
40 *Al-Mu'minūn*, 10–11.

PRAYER TWENTY ONE

اللَّهُمَّ صَلِّ وَسَلِّمْ عَلَى سَيِّدِنَا مُحَمَّدٍ الْبَشِيرِ الْمُبَشِّرِ لِلْمُصَلِّينَ بِمَا قَالَ اللهُ الْعَظِيم
﴿إِنَّ ٱللَّهَ وَمَلَٰٓئِكَتَهُۥ يُصَلُّونَ عَلَى ٱلنَّبِيِّۚ يَٰٓأَيُّهَا ٱلَّذِينَ ءَامَنُواْ صَلُّواْ
عَلَيۡهِ وَسَلِّمُواْ تَسۡلِيمًا ٥٦﴾ ﴿يُؤۡتِكُمۡ كِفۡلَيۡنِ مِن رَّحۡمَتِهِۦ وَيَجۡعَل
لَّكُمۡ نُورٗا تَمۡشُونَ بِهِۦ وَيَغۡفِرۡ لَكُمۡۚ وَٱللَّهُ غَفُورٞ رَّحِيمٞ ٢٨﴾.

O Allah, send mercy and peace upon our master Muhammad, the bearer of good news, who conveys Your joyous tidings to all who invoke blessings upon him: "Indeed, Allah showers His blessings upon the Prophet, and His angels pray for him. O believers! Invoke Allah's blessings upon him and salute him with worthy greetings of peace;"[41] "and He will grant you a double share of His mercy, provide you with a light to help you walk, and forgive you; for Allah is All-Forgiving, Most Merciful."[42]

41 *Al-Aḥzāb*, 56.
42 *Al-Ḥadīd*, 28.

PRAYER TWENTY TWO

اللَّهُمَّ صَلِّ وَسَلِّمْ عَلَى سَيِّدِنَا مُحَمَّدٍ الْبَشِيرِ الْمُبَشِّرِ لِلْمُبَشِّرِينَ بِمَا قَالَ اللهُ الْعَظِيم
﴿وَبَشِّرِ ٱلَّذِينَ ءَامَنُوا۟ وَعَمِلُوا۟ ٱلصَّٰلِحَٰتِ ٢٥﴾ ﴿لَهُمُ ٱلْبُشْرَىٰ فِى
ٱلْحَيَوٰةِ ٱلدُّنْيَا وَفِى ٱلْءَاخِرَةِ ۚ لَا تَبْدِيلَ لِكَلِمَٰتِ ٱللَّهِ ۚ ذَٰلِكَ هُوَ ٱلْفَوْزُ
ٱلْعَظِيمُ ٦٤﴾.

O Allah, send mercy and peace upon our master Muhammad, the bearer of good news, who conveys Your joyous tidings to those who proclaim them: "Give good news to those who believe and do good;"[43] "for them is good news in this worldly life and the Hereafter. There is no change in the promise of Allah. That is truly the ultimate triumph."[44]

43 *Al-Baqarah*, 25.
44 *Yūnus*, 64.

PRAYER TWENTY THREE

اللَّهُمَّ صَلِّ وَسَلِّمْ عَلَى سَيِّدِنَا مُحَمَّدٍ الْبَشِيرِ الْمُبَشِّرِ لِلْفَائِزِينَ بِمَا قَالَ اللهُ الْعَظِيم

﴿وَمَن يُطِعِ ٱللَّهَ وَرَسُولَهُۥ فَقَدْ فَازَ فَوْزًا عَظِيمًا ۝٧١﴾.

O Allah, send mercy and peace upon our master Muhammad, the bearer of good news, who conveys Your joyous tidings to the triumphant: "And whoever obeys Allah and His Messenger has truly achieved a great triumph."[45]

45 *Al-Aḥzāb*, 71.

PRAYER TWENTY FOUR

اللَّهُمَّ صَلِّ وَسَلِّمْ عَلَى سَيِّدِنَا مُحَمَّدٍ الْبَشِيرِ الْمُبَشِّرِ لِلزَّاهِدِينَ بِمَا قَالَ اللهُ الْعَظِيم
﴿ٱلْمَالُ وَٱلْبَنُونَ زِينَةُ ٱلْحَيَوٰةِ ٱلدُّنْيَا ۖ وَٱلْبَٰقِيَٰتُ ٱلصَّٰلِحَٰتُ خَيْرٌ عِندَ
رَبِّكَ ثَوَابًا وَخَيْرٌ أَمَلًا ﴿٤٦﴾﴾.

O Allah, send mercy and peace upon our master Muhammad, the bearer of good news, who conveys Your joyous tidings to those detached from worldly vanities: "Wealth and children are the adornment of this worldly life, but everlasting good deeds are far better with your Lord in reward and in hope."[46]

46 *Al-Kahf*, 46.

PRAYER TWENTY FIVE

اللَّهُمَّ صَلِّ وَسَلِّمْ عَلَىٰ سَيِّدِنَا مُحَمَّدٍ الْبَشِيرِ الْمُبَشِّرِ لِلْأُمِّيِّينَ بِمَا قَالَ اللهُ الْعَظِيمُ
﴿كُنْتُمْ خَيْرَ أُمَّةٍ أُخْرِجَتْ لِلنَّاسِ تَأْمُرُونَ بِالْمَعْرُوفِ وَتَنْهَوْنَ عَنِ
الْمُنْكَرِ ﴿١١٠﴾﴾.

O Allah, send mercy and peace upon our master Muhammad, the bearer of good news, who conveys Your joyous tidings to the unlettered: "You are the best community ever raised for humanity – you encourage good and forbid evil."[47]

47 *Āl ʿImrān*, 110.

PRAYER TWENTY SIX

اللَّهُمَّ صَلِّ وَسَلِّمْ عَلَى سَيِّدِنَا مُحَمَّدٍ الْبَشِيرِ الْمُبَشِّرِ لِلْمُصْطَفَيْنَ بِمَا قَالَ اللهُ الْعَظِيم
﴿ثُمَّ أَوْرَثْنَا ٱلْكِتَٰبَ ٱلَّذِينَ ٱصْطَفَيْنَا مِنْ عِبَادِنَا ۖ فَمِنْهُمْ ظَالِمٌ لِّنَفْسِهِۦ
وَمِنْهُم مُّقْتَصِدٌ وَمِنْهُمْ سَابِقٌۢ بِٱلْخَيْرَٰتِ بِإِذْنِ ٱللَّهِ ۚ ذَٰلِكَ هُوَ ٱلْفَضْلُ
ٱلْكَبِيرُ ٣٢﴾.

O Allah, send mercy and peace upon our master Muhammad, the bearer of good news, who conveys Your joyous tidings to those You have chosen: "Then We granted the Book to those We have chosen from Our servants. Some of them wrong themselves, some follow a middle course, and some are foremost in good deeds by Allah's will. That is truly the greatest bounty."[48]

48 *Fāṭir*, 32.

PRAYER TWENTY SEVEN

اللَّهُمَّ صَلِّ وَسَلِّمْ عَلَى سَيِّدِنَا مُحَمَّدٍ الْبَشِيرِ الْمُبَشِّرِ لِلْمُذْنِبِينَ بِمَا قَالَ اللهُ الْعَظِيم
﴿قُلْ يَٰعِبَادِىَ ٱلَّذِينَ أَسْرَفُوا۟ عَلَىٰٓ أَنفُسِهِمْ لَا تَقْنَطُوا۟ مِن رَّحْمَةِ ٱللَّهِ ۚ إِنَّ
ٱللَّهَ يَغْفِرُ ٱلذُّنُوبَ جَمِيعًا ۚ إِنَّهُۥ هُوَ ٱلْغَفُورُ ٱلرَّحِيمُ ﴿٥٣﴾﴾.

O Allah, send mercy and peace upon our master Muhammad, the bearer of good news, who conveys Your joyous tidings to those who have sinned: "Say, 'O my servants who have exceeded the limits against their souls! Do not lose hope in Allah's mercy, for Allah certainly forgives all sins. He is indeed the All-Forgiving, Most Merciful.'"[49]

49 *Al-Zumar*, 53.

PRAYER TWENTY EIGHT

اللَّهُمَّ صَلِّ وَسَلِّمْ عَلَى سَيِّدِنَا مُحَمَّدٍ الْبَشِيرِ الْمُبَشِّرِ لِلْمُسْتَغْفِرِينَ بِمَا قَالَ اللهُ الْعَظِيم
﴿وَمَن يَعْمَلْ سُوٓءًا أَوْ يَظْلِمْ نَفْسَهُۥ ثُمَّ يَسْتَغْفِرِ ٱللَّهَ يَجِدِ ٱللَّهَ غَفُورًا
رَّحِيمًا ١١٠﴾.

O Allah, send mercy and peace upon our master Muhammad, the bearer of good news, who conveys Your joyous tidings to those who ask for Your forgiveness: "Whoever commits evil or wrongs themselves then seeks Allah's forgiveness will certainly find Allah All-Forgiving, Most Merciful."[50]

---

50 *Al-Nisā'*, 110.

PRAYER TWENTY NINE

اللَّهُمَّ صَلِّ وَسَلِّمْ عَلَى سَيِّدِنَا مُحَمَّدٍ الْبَشِيرِ الْمُبَشِّرِ لِلْعَابِدِينَ بِمَا قَالَ اللهُ الْعَظِيم
﴿إِنَّ ٱلَّذِينَ سَبَقَتۡ لَهُم مِّنَّا ٱلۡحُسۡنَىٰٓ أُوْلَٰٓئِكَ عَنۡهَا مُبۡعَدُونَ ١٠١
لَا يَسۡمَعُونَ حَسِيسَهَاۖ وَهُمۡ فِي مَا ٱشۡتَهَتۡ أَنفُسُهُمۡ خَٰلِدُونَ ١٠٢ لَا
يَحۡزُنُهُمُ ٱلۡفَزَعُ ٱلۡأَكۡبَرُ وَتَتَلَقَّىٰهُمُ ٱلۡمَلَٰٓئِكَةُ هَٰذَا يَوۡمُكُمُ ٱلَّذِي
كُنتُمۡ تُوعَدُونَ ١٠٣﴾.

O Allah, send mercy and peace upon our master Muhammad, the bearer of good news, who conveys Your joyous tidings to those who adore You and drawn near to You in humble worship: "Surely those for whom We have destined the finest reward will be kept far away from Hell, not even hearing the slightest hissing from it. And they will delight forever in what their souls desire. The Supreme Terror will not disturb them, and the angels will greet them: 'This is your Day, which you have been promised.'"[51]

---

51 *Al-Anbiyā'*, 101–103.

PRAYER THIRTY

اللَّهُمَّ صَلِّ وَسَلِّمْ عَلَى سَيِّدِنَا مُحَمَّدٍ الْبَشِيرِ الْمُبَشِّرِ لِلْمُؤْمِنِينَ بِمَا قَالَ اللهُ الْعَظِيمِ ﴿إِنَّ
ٱلْمُسْلِمِينَ وَٱلْمُسْلِمَٰتِ وَٱلْمُؤْمِنِينَ وَٱلْمُؤْمِنَٰتِ وَٱلْقَٰنِتِينَ وَٱلْقَٰنِتَٰتِ
وَٱلصَّٰدِقِينَ وَٱلصَّٰدِقَٰتِ وَٱلصَّٰبِرِينَ وَٱلصَّٰبِرَٰتِ وَٱلْخَٰشِعِينَ
وَٱلْخَٰشِعَٰتِ وَٱلْمُتَصَدِّقِينَ وَٱلْمُتَصَدِّقَٰتِ وَٱلصَّٰٓئِمِينَ وَٱلصَّٰٓئِمَٰتِ
وَٱلْحَٰفِظِينَ فُرُوجَهُمْ وَٱلْحَٰفِظَٰتِ وَٱلذَّٰكِرِينَ ٱللَّهَ كَثِيرًا وَٱلذَّٰكِرَٰتِ
أَعَدَّ ٱللَّهُ لَهُم مَّغْفِرَةً وَأَجْرًا عَظِيمًا ﴿٣٥﴾﴾ ﴿وَأَن لَّيْسَ لِلْإِنسَٰنِ إِلَّا مَا
سَعَىٰ ﴿٣٩﴾ وَأَنَّ سَعْيَهُۥ سَوْفَ يُرَىٰ ﴿٤٠﴾ ثُمَّ يُجْزَىٰهُ ٱلْجَزَآءَ ٱلْأَوْفَىٰ ﴿٤١﴾ وَأَنَّ
إِلَىٰ رَبِّكَ ٱلْمُنتَهَىٰ ﴿٤٢﴾﴾.

O Allah, send mercy and peace upon our master Muhammad, the bearer of good news, who conveys Your joyous tidings to Muslims entirely: "Surely, Muslim men and women, believing men and women, devout men and women, truthful men and women, patient men and women, humble men and women, charitable men and women, fasting men and women, men and women who guard their chastity, and men and women who remember Allah often – for all of them Allah has prepared forgiveness and a great reward;"[52] and "that each person will only have what they endeavoured towards, and that their endeavours will be seen, then they will be fully rewarded, and that to your Lord alone is the ultimate return of all things."[53]

52 *Al-Aḥzāb*, 35.
53 *Al-Najm*, 39–42.

A FINAL PRAYER

اللَّهُمَّ صَلِّ عَلَيْهِ صَلَاةً تَشْرَحُ بِهَا صُدُورًا وَتَهُونُ بِهَا الأُمُورُ وَتَنْكَشِفُ
بِهَا السُّتُورُ وَسَلِّمْ تَسْلِيمًا كَثِيرًا دَائِمًا إِلَى يَوْمِ الدِّينِ ﴿دَعْوَاهُمْ فِيهَا
سُبْحَانَكَ اللَّهُمَّ وَتَحِيَّتُهُمْ فِيهَا سَلَامٌ ۚ وَآخِرُ دَعْوَاهُمْ أَنِ الْحَمْدُ لِلَّهِ
رَبِّ الْعَالَمِينَ ١٠﴾.

O Allah, grace him with a mercy whereby hearts are opened, difficulties relieved, and veils lifted; and send him peace abundant and abiding until the Day of Judgement: "Their prayer will be, 'Glory be to You, O Allah!' and their greeting will be, 'Peace!' and their closing prayer will be, 'All praise is for Allah – Lord of all Worlds!'"[54]

54 *Yūnus*, 10.

The Obligation and Virtue of Sending Blessings and Salutations Upon the Prophet ﷺ

By Qāḍī ʿIyāḍ al-Yaḥṣubī

Allah Exalted says: "Indeed, Allah showers His Blessings upon the Prophet, and His Angels pray for him. O believers! Invoke the Blessings of Allah upon him, and salute him with worthy greetings of peace."[1]

Ibn ʿAbbās ؓ said: "It means: 'Indeed, Allah and His Angels send blessings[2] upon the Prophet ﷺ.'"[3]

Others interpreted the verse to mean: "Indeed, Allah has mercy upon the Prophet ﷺ, and His Angels supplicate for him."

Al-Mubarrad said: "The root meaning of *ṣalāh* is 'to have mercy'. From Allah this is mercy, and from the Angels this is gentleness and supplicating for Allah to have mercy [upon him]."

In the narration describing the supplications of the Angels for a person who sits waiting for the prayer, they are related as saying: "O Allah, forgive him. O Allah, have mercy on him."[4]

Bakr al-Qushayrī commented: "'*Ṣalāh*' from Allah Exalted to any person other than the Prophet ﷺ is mercy, and to the Prophet ﷺ is distinction and increased honour."[5]

---

1 *al-Aḥzāb*, 56.
2 Translator's note: The word in the verse above is "*yuṣallūn*", which would normally mean "they pray", which is why this explanation is necessary.
3 Related by Ibn Jarīr from Ibn Abī Ḥātim. See *Al-Manāhil*, p. 1046.
4 Reported by Bukhārī (659) and Muslim (649/272) from Abū Hurayrah.
5 Related by Ibn Ḥajar in *Fatḥ al-Bārī* (11/156) from the present author.

Abū al-ʿĀliyah[6] said: "'*Ṣalāh*' from Allah is His Praise upon the Prophet ﷺ to the Angels, and from the Angels is supplication."

Qāḍī Abū al-Faḍl remarked: "In the narration where he taught how to send blessings upon him, the Prophet ﷺ distinguished between the words '*ṣalāh*' and '*barakah*', which suggests that they have two separate meanings."

As for the "worthy greetings of peace" or "salutations" that Allah Exalted commanded His servants to send upon the Prophet ﷺ, Qāḍī Abū Bakr ibn Bukayr said: "This verse was sent down to the Messenger of Allah ﷺ, and Allah commanded his Companions to send salutations upon him. Likewise, those after them are commanded to send salutations upon the Prophet ﷺ when they visit his grave and when they mention him."

There are three views on the meaning of the word "*salām*" (translated above as "salutations").

The first potential meaning is: safety (*salāmah*) for you and with you. According to this view, "*salām*" is the present participle, as is the case with "*ladhādh*" and "*ladhādhah*" ("delectable" and "delectation").

The second possibility is that the "*salām*" is the one responsible for your protection and care; a guardian and guarantor. This is the case with al-Salām, one of the Names of Allah.

The third meaning of "*salām*" is conciliation and submission. As Allah Exalted said: "But no! By your Lord, they will never be [true] believers until they accept you [O Prophet] as the judge in their disputes, and find no resistance within themselves against your decision and submit (*yusallimū*) wholeheartedly."[7]

THE RULING OF SENDING BLESSINGS UPON THE PROPHET ﷺ

Know that sending blessings upon the Prophet ﷺ is a general obligation, [although] not restricted by time, because of the command of Allah Exalted to send blessings upon him, and the scholars and imams unanimously agreed that it is an obligatory act.

Abū Jaʿfar Muhammad ibn Jarīr al-Ṭabarī رحمه الله said that the verse only carries the act to a recommended status, and he also claimed unanimity for that view. Perhaps he was referring to sending blessings

---

6 Rufayʿ ibn Mihrān al-Riyāḥī.

7 *al-Nisā'*, 65.

upon the Prophet ﷺ more than once, whereas the obligation which absolutely must be fulfilled to avoid sin or harm is to send blessings upon him once, for example by bearing witness to his Prophethood. Anything beyond that is recommended and highly desirable, and is one of the Sunnahs of Islam and slogans of its people.

Qāḍī Abū al-Ḥasan ibn al-Qaṣṣār[8] said: "The well-known view from our companions is that this is a general obligation upon humankind, and that it is mandatory upon each person to do it [at least] once in their lifetime, so long as they are able."

Qāḍī Abū Bakr ibn Bukayr commented: "Allah made it mandatory for His creation to invoke the Blessings of Allah upon His Prophet ﷺ and salute him with worthy greetings of peace. He did not set a known time for that, so the obligation is for a man to do this abundantly and not be negligent in doing so."

Qāḍī Abū Muhammad ibn Naṣr[9] stated: "Sending blessings upon the Prophet ﷺ is a general obligation."

Qāḍī Abū ʿAbdillāh Muhammad ibn Saʿīd remarked: "Mālik, his companions, and other people of knowledge said that sending blessings upon the Prophet ﷺ is a general obligation tied to the covenant of faith and is not reserved to prayer, and that the obligation is dropped when a person sends blessings upon him once."

The companions of Shāfiʿī said: "The obligation that Allah Exalted and His Messenger ﷺ commanded is within the prayer." They added: "As for outside of that, there is no doubt that it is not mandatory."

As for within the prayer, the two imams Abū Jaʿfar ibn Jarīr al-Ṭabarī and al-Ṭaḥāwī and others cited a consensus amongst early and later leading scholars that sending blessings upon the Prophet ﷺ in the *tashahhud* is not obligatory.[10]

---

8 Shaykh of the Mālikīs, ʿAlī ibn ʿUmar ibn Aḥmad al-Baghdādī ibn al-Qaṣṣār; an expert in the principles of jurisprudence. He passed away in 397 AH. His biography can be found in *Siyar Aʿlām al-Nubalā'* (17/107-108).

9 The imam, esteemed scholar, and Shaykh of the Mālikīs, ʿAbd al-Wahhāb ibn ʿAlī ibn Naṣr al-Taghlibī. He passed away in 422 AH. His biography can be found in *Siyar Aʿlām al-Nubalā'* (17/429-432).

10 Ibn Kathīr said in his exegesis of Sūrah al-Aḥzāb: "There is no consensus upon this difference (i.e., to the view of Shāfiʿī), neither in the past nor recently." Sending blessings upon the Prophet ﷺ after the *tashahhud* being obligatory was the view adopted by ʿUmar ibn al-Khaṭṭāb, his son ʿAbdullāh, Ibn Masʿūd,

Shāfiʿī was the exception to this. He said: "Whoever does not send blessings upon the Prophet ﷺ between the end of the final *tashahhud* and the *taslīm*, his prayer is null and void. Saying it before that is not permitted." However, there is no precedence to this statement and no Sunnah to back it up. He went to extremes in his criticism of this issue by contradicting those who came before him, and he was censured by a group of scholars including Ṭabarī, Qushayrī, and others.

Abū Bakr ibn al-Mundhir[11] said: "It is recommended for no-one to perform a prayer without invoking blessings upon the Messenger of Allah ﷺ. If someone misses that, then their prayer is still acceptable according to the *madhhab* of Mālik, the people of Madinah, Sufyān al-Thawrī, and the people of Kufa, including rationalists and others, and this was the view of many people of knowledge."

It was reported from Mālik and Sufyān that they considered it to be recommended in the final *tashahhud*, and the person who leaves it out has done something offensive. Shāfiʿī was an exception, saying that a person who leaves it out must repeat their prayer. Isḥāq[12] also considered repeating the prayer necessary, but only if a person leaves it out intentionally, not if they do so forgetfully.

Abū Muhammad ibn Abī Zayd[13] reported from Muhammad ibn al-Mawwāz[14] that sending blessings upon the Prophet ﷺ is obligatory. Abū Muhammad said, "He does not mean one of the obligatory acts

---

Abū Masʿūd al-Badrī, Jābir ibn Zayd, al-Shaʿbī, Muhammad ibn Kaʿb al-Quraẓī, Shāfiʿī, Aḥmad ibn Ḥanbal, Isḥāq ibn Rāhawayh, and Ibn al-Mawwāz, and it was the opinion preferred by Qāḍī Abū Bakr ibn al-ʿArabī. And many said it was not obligatory, including Mālik, Abū Ḥanīfah, his companions, al-Thawrī, al-Awzāʿī, and others. See *Tafsīr Ibn Kathīr* (3/508), *Fatḥ al-Bārī* (11/164), and the comments of *Al-Taʿlīq al-Mughnī ʿalā al-Dāraquṭnī* (1/356).

11 The imam, *ḥāfiẓ*, and esteemed scholar, Muhammad ibn Ibrāhīm ibn al-Mundhir al-Nīsābūrī. He is counted amongst the Shāfiʿī jurists. He passed away in 318 AH. His biography can be found in *Siyar Aʿlām al-Nubalā'* (14/290-292).

12 Ibn Rāhawayh.

13 Eminent scholar of the Maghreb, ʿAbdullāh ibn Abī Zayd. He was known as "Mālik al-Ṣaghīr", or "the little Mālik". He passed away in 389 AH. His biography can be found in *Siyar Aʿlām al-Nubalā'* (17/10).

14 The imam, esteemed scholar, and jurist, Muhammad ibn Ibrāhīm ibn Ziyād al-Iskandarānī al-Mālikī. He passed away in 269 AH. His biography can be found in *Siyar Aʿlām al-Nubalā'* (13/6).

of the prayer", and the same was said by Muhammad ibn ʿAbd al-Ḥakam[15] and others.

Ibn al-Qaṣṣār[16] and ʿAbd al-Wahhāb[17] reported that Muhammad ibn al-Mawwāz considered it an obligation of the prayer, like the opinion of Shāfiʿī.

Abū Yaʿlā al-ʿAbdī al-Mālikī said that there are three opinions in the [Mālikī] *madhhab* regarding sending blessings upon the Messenger of Allah ﷺ in the prayer: that it is an obligation, recommended, or a Sunnah.

Al-Khaṭṭābī and other companions of Shāfiʿī differed with Shāfiʿī on this issue. Al-Khaṭṭābī said: "It is not an obligatory act in prayer. This is the view of the majority of jurisprudents except Shāfiʿī, and I do not know of any precedence for his view."

The evidence that it is not one of the obligatory acts of prayer is the practice of the righteous predecessors before Shāfiʿī and their consensus on the issue. The people severely criticized Shāfiʿī on this point. [However,] it was the *tashahhud* of Ibn Masʿūd[18] that was chosen by Shāfiʿī[19], which Ibn Masʿūd was taught by the Prophet ﷺ and did not include an invocation of blessings upon him. Likewise, the *tashahhud*s narrated from the Prophet ﷺ by Abū Hurayrah,[20] Ibn ʿAbbās,[21] Jābir,[22] Ibn ʿUmar,[23] Abū Saʿīd al-Khudrī,[24] Abū Mūsā

---

15 The Mālikī jurist, imam, and esteemed scholar, Muhammad ibn ʿAbdillāh ibn ʿAbd al-Ḥakam. He was born in 182 AH and died in 268 AH. His biography can be found in *Siyar Aʿlām al-Nubalā'* (12/497-501).

16 Qāḍī Abū al-Ḥasan ibn al-Qaṣṣār.

17 Qāḍī Abū Muhammad ibn Naṣr.

18 Reported by Bukhārī (831) and Muslim (402).

19 Shāfiʿī actually preferred the *tashahhud* of Ibn ʿAbbās. Imam Nawawī states in *Al-Adhkar*, in the notes to hadith no. 182: "And the best of them (i.e., *tashahhuds*) according to Shāfiʿī was the narration of Ibn ʿAbbās, due to the extra blessed words it contains."

20 Reported by Ibn Mardawayh. See *Al-Manāhil*, p. 1048.

21 Reported by Muslim (403).

22 Reported by Nasā'ī (2/243) and Bayhaqī (2/142). Authenticated by Ḥākim (1/267), and Dhahabī concurred. Tirmidhī said, as related in the *Sunan* of Bayhaqī (2/142): "I asked Bukhārī about this narration, and he said: 'False.'"

23 Reported by Abū Dāwūd (971), and its chain is *ṣaḥīḥ*.

24 Reported by Ibn Mardawayh. See *Al-Manāhil*, p. 1048.

al-Ashʿarī,²⁵ and ʿAbdullāh ibn al-Zubayr²⁶ do not mention sending blessings upon the Prophet ﷺ.

Ibn ʿAbbās and Jābir narrated, "The Prophet ﷺ used to teach us the *tashahhud* like he taught us a *sūrah* of the Qurʾan,"²⁷ and Abū Saʿīd narrated something similar.²⁸

Ibn ʿUmar narrated: "Abū Bakr used to teach us the *tashahhud* from the pulpit just as children are taught the Book."²⁹ ʿUmar ؓ also used to teach the *tashahhud* from the pulpit.³⁰

In another narration, the Prophet ﷺ said: "There is no prayer for the one who does not send blessings upon me."³¹

Ibn al-Qaṣṣār commented: "Meaning: no complete prayer. Or, [it is referring to] a person who does not send blessings upon him even once in their lifetime." Furthermore, the scholars of hadith all declared the transmissions of this narration to be weak.

---

25 Reported by Muslim (404).
26 Reported by Bazzār (562) and by Ṭabarānī in *Al-Kabīr*. Mentioned by Haythamī in *Majmaʿ al-Zawāʾid* (2/141), where he said: "The transmission revolves around Ibn Lahīʿah, whom there is some discussion regarding." Suyūṭī said in *Al-Manāhil*, p. 1048, following the statement of Ibn Ḥajar in *al-Talkhīṣ al-Ḥabīr* (1/268): "It was also related by other Companions, up to a total of twenty-four."
27 The narration of Ibn ʿAbbās was reported by Muslim (403), and the narration of Jābir was reported by Nasāʾī (2/243) and Bayhaqī (2/142).
28 It was also narrated by Ibn Masʿūd and Jarīr ibn ʿAbdillāh, as mentioned in *Majmaʿ al-Zawāʾid* (2/140, 141).
29 Reported by Ibn Abī Shaybah, as mentioned in *al-Talkhīṣ al-Ḥabīr*. Ibn Ḥajar said: "It was related by Abū Bakr ibn Mardawayh in *Kitāb al-Tashahhud* in a *marfūʿ* narration from Abū Bakr, and its chain is *ḥasan*." Also reported by Ṭabarānī in *Al-Kabīr* from Ibn ʿUmar, with the wording: "The Prophet ﷺ used to teach the people the *tashahhud* from the pulpit, just as a teacher educates their students." Haythamī said in *Majmaʿ al-Zawāʾid* (2/140): "Its chain contains ʿAbd al-Raḥmān ibn Isḥāq Abū Shaybah, who is a weak narrator."
30 Reported by Mālik in *Al-Muwaṭṭaʾ* (1/90) and Bayhaqī (2/142). Authenticated by Ḥākim (1/266), and Dhahabī concurred. Also authenticated by Nawawī in *Al-Adhkar*, hadith no. 180. See *al-Talkhīṣ al-Ḥabīr* (1/265).
31 Reported by Ibn Mājah (400), Ḥākim (1/269), Bayhaqī (2/379) and Dāraquṭnī (1/355) from Sahl ibn Saʿd al-Sāʿidī. Its chain contains ʿAbd al-Muhaymin ibn ʿAbbās. Bayhaqī said: "He is a weak narrator and his transmissions should not be used as evidence." See *al-Talkhīṣ al-Ḥabīr* (1/262).

Abū Jaʿfar narrated from Abū Masʿūd that the Prophet ﷺ said: "Whoever performs a prayer in which they neither send blessings up me nor upon my family, their prayer will not be accepted from them."[32]

Dāraquṭnī said: "The most accurate view is found in the statement of Abū Jaʿfar Muhammad ibn ʿAlī ibn al-Ḥusayn: 'If I performed a prayer in which I did not invoke blessings upon the Prophet ﷺ or his family, I would consider that prayer incomplete.'"[33]

PLACES IN WHICH INVOKING BLESSINGS UPON THE PROPHET ﷺ IS RECOMMENDED AND DESIRABLE

As we have previously mentioned, this includes sending blessings upon the Prophet ﷺ during the *tashahhud* of prayer, which should be done after the final *tashahhud* and before supplication.

I read the following hadith to Abū ʿAlī al-Qāḍī, who narrated from Imam Abū al-Qāsim al-Balkhī, from al-Fārisī, from Abū al-Qāsim al-Khuzāʿī, from Abū Saʿīd al-Haytham ibn Kulayb, from Abū ʿĪsā al-Ḥāfiẓ, from Maḥmūd ibn Ghaylān, from ʿAbdullāh ibn Yazīd al-Muqri', from Ḥaywah ibn Shurayḥ, from Abū Hānī' al-Khawlānī, that ʿAmr ibn Mālik al-Janbī informed him that he heard Faḍālah ibn ʿUbayd say: "The Prophet ﷺ heard a man supplicating in his prayer without sending blessings upon the Prophet ﷺ. The Prophet ﷺ said: 'This man has rushed.' Then, he called him over and said to him and others: 'When you pray, start by praising and extolling Allah. Then, let them send blessings upon the Prophet ﷺ, and then supplicate after that for whatever they wish."[34]

From another chain of transmission, the narration reads, "…by glorifying Allah", and that is more accurate.

---

32 Reported by Dāraquṭnī (1/355) and others from Jābir al-Juʿfī, from Abū Jaʿfar, from Abū Masʿūd al-Anṣārī (ʿUqbah ibn ʿAmr al-Badrī) in a *marfūʿ* narration. Dāraquṭnī said: "Jābir is a weak narrator, and there was some difference of opinion regarding him." See also the narration that follows.

33 Reported by Dāraquṭnī (1/355-356) and others from Jābir al-Juʿfī, from Abū Jaʿfar Muhammad ibn ʿAlī ibn al-Ḥusayn, from Abū Masʿūd al-Anṣārī, from his own words, and not from the statement of Muhammad ibn ʿAlī ibn al-Ḥusayn.

34 Reported here from Tirmidhī (3477). Also reported by Abū Dāwūd (1481) and Nasā'ī (3/44). Tirmidhī said: "This hadith is *ḥasan ṣaḥīḥ*." Its referencing can be found in *Bulūgh al-Marām* (311) with my commentary.

ʿUmar ibn al-Khaṭṭāb ﷺ narrated: "Supplication and prayer are suspended between Heaven and Earth, and none of them ascend to Allah until blessings have been sent upon the Prophet ﷺ."[35]

ʿAlī ibn Abī Ṭālib ﷺ narrated the same meaning from the Prophet ﷺ, adding: "...and upon the family of Muhammad."[36]

It was also related that supplications are blocked until the supplicator sends blessings upon the Prophet ﷺ.[37]

Ibn Masʿūd ﷺ narrated: "If one of you wishes to ask Allah for something, they should begin by praising and extolling Him as He deserves, and then send blessings upon the Prophet ﷺ. Then, they may ask, for that is more likely to succeed.[38]"[39]

Jābir ﷺ narrated: "The Messenger of Allah ﷺ said: 'Do not make me like a rider's vessel, for a rider fills his vessel and then sets it down and lifts up their luggage. If he needs a drink, he drinks from it, and if he needs to perform ablution, he performs ablution from it. Otherwise, he pours it away. Instead, put me in the beginning, the middle, and the end of supplications.'"[40]

---

35 Reported by Tirmidhī (486) without the phrase: "and prayer". See the comments of esteemed scholar Aḥmad Shākir, and *Al-Qawl al-Badīʿ*, p. 321.

36 Reported by Abū al-Shaykh in *Al-Thawāb* and Bayhaqī in *Shuʿab al-Īmān*. See *Al-Manāhil*, p. 1055. Graded *ḥasan* by Suyūṭī in *Al-Jāmiʿ al-Ṣaghīr* (4266). Reported by Ṭabarānī in *Al-Awsaṭ* in a *mawqūf* narration from ʿAlī. Haythamī said in *Majmaʿ al-Zawāʾid* (10/160): "Its narrators are reliable." Mundhirī said in *Al-Targhīb wa al-Tarhīb* (2/505): "Related by Ṭabarānī in *Al-Awsaṭ* in a *mawqūf* narration, and its transmitters are reliable. Some said that it is a *marfūʿ* narration, but the *mawqūf* is more accurate."

37 Reported by Daylamī in *Musnad al-Firdaws* from Anas, as found in *Tuḥfah al-Dhākirīn*, p. 51. Shawkānī said: "Its chain contains Muhammad ibn ʿAbd al-ʿAzīz al-Daynawrī." Dhahabī said in *Al-Ḍuʿafāʾ*: "His narrations are odd (*munkar*)."

38 i.e., in achieving their request.

39 Reported by Maʿmar ibn Rāshid in *Al-Jāmiʿ* (19642) from the transmission of ʿAbd al-Razzāq. Mentioned by Haythamī in *Majmaʿ al-Zawāʾid* (10/155), where he said: "It was related by Ṭabarānī and its narrators are *ṣaḥīḥ*, except that Abū ʿUbaydah did not hear from his father." Mentioned again by Haythamī (10/160), where he said: "It is a good (*jayyid*) hadith." Suyūṭī authenticated its chain in *Al-Manāhil*, p. 1056.

40 Reported by Bazzār (3156), ʿAbd al-Razzāq (3117), Abū Yaʿlā, Bayhaqī in *Shuʿab al-Īmān*, and others. Haythamī said in *Majmaʿ al-Zawāʾid* (10/155): "Its chain contains Mūsā ibn ʿUbaydah, who is a weak narrator." Ibn Ḥajar said in *Takhrīj*

Ibn ʿAṭā' commented: "Supplication has pillars, wings, means, and times. If you conform to its pillars, it will be strong. If you conform to its wings, it will soar in the sky. If you conform to its times, it will succeed. If you conform to its means, it will accomplish [the thing you are asking for]. Its pillars are presence of the heart, gentleness, submission, humility, connection of the heart to Allah, and its disconnection from [relying on] other means. Its wings are sincerity. Its times are the early mornings. And its means are invoking blessings upon the Prophet Muhammad ﷺ."

In one narration, the Prophet ﷺ said: "Supplications between two blessings invoked upon me are never rejected."[41]

And in another narration, he said: "Every supplication is blocked beneath the sky. When a blessing upon me arrives, the supplication ascends."[42]

At the end of the supplication of Ibn ʿAbbās related from him by Ḥanash, he said: "Respond to my supplication!" Then, he began by invoking blessings upon the Prophet Muhammad ﷺ, saying: "O Allah, I ask You to bless Muhammad, Your slave, Prophet, Messenger, with the best blessings You have sent upon anyone from Your entire creation. Āmīn."[43]

In other times, blessings should be sent upon the Prophet ﷺ when he is mentioned, his name is heard or spoken[44], and with the call to prayer.

---

al-Adhkār, "A *gharīb* hadith", and Sakhāwī followed him in *Al-Qawl al-Badīʿ*, p. 319. See also *Jāmiʿ al-Uṣūl* (4/155).

41 As stated by Sakhāwī in *Al-Qawl al-Badīʿ*, p. 321, this narration is found in *Sharaf al-Muṣṭafā* without a chain of transmission.

42 Related in a similar form by Ibn al-Athīr in *Jāmiʿ al-Uṣūl* (2121) from ʿUmar ibn al-Khaṭṭāb in a *marfūʿ* narration. He said: "This transmission was mentioned by Razīn." Also reported by Tirmidhī (486) from ʿUmar in a *mawqūf* narration. See also *Al-Qawl al-Badīʿ*, p. 320.

43 The complete supplication is mentioned by Sakhāwī in *Al-Qawl al-Badīʿ*, pp. 337-338. He said: "It was related by Tirmidhī."

44 In another manuscript: "...or written."

The Prophet ﷺ said: "May his nose be rubbed in dust,[45] a man in whose presence I am mentioned and does not send blessings upon me."[46]

Ibn Ḥabīb[47] disliked for the Prophet ﷺ to be mentioned at the time of slaughtering an animal.

Saḥnūn disliked invoking blessings upon the Prophet ﷺ at times of shock or amazement. He said: "Invoking blessings upon him should only be done in a contented manner and seeking its reward."

Aṣbagh[48] related from Ibn al-Qāsim: "Times that only Allah should be mentioned: when slaughtering animals, and when sneezing. [In these contexts,] do not say, after mentioning Allah, 'Muhammad is the Messenger of Allah.' However, if you said, after mentioning Allah, 'May Allah send His blessings upon Muhammad', that does not count as naming him alongside Allah."

Ashhab[49] adopted the same position, saying: "It is not appropriate to make sending blessings upon the Prophet ﷺ a Sunnah of those situations."[50]

Nasā'ī related from Aws ibn Aws that the Prophet ﷺ instructed increasing in sending blessings upon him on Fridays.[51]

---

45 The word here for "rubbed in dust" is "*raghima*", but Ibn al-ʿArabī said that it should be "*raghama*". The meaning is: "May he be humiliated." See *Al-Targhīb wa al-Tarhīb* (2/508).

46 Reported by Tirmidhī (3545) and Ḥākim (1/549). Tirmidhī said: "This hadith is *ḥasan gharīb*." See also *Mawārid al-Ẓam'ān* (2028).

47 The scholar of Andalusia, ʿAbd al-Malik ibn Ḥabīb al-Qurṭubī al-Mālikī. He was born during the life of Imam Mālik, after 170 AH, and passed away in either 238 or 239 AH. His biography can be found in *Siyar Aʿlām al-Nubalā'* (12/102-107).

48 The mufti and scholar of Egypt, Aṣbagh ibn al-Faraj al-Mālikī. He was born after 150 AH and died in 225 AH. His biography can be found in *Siyar Aʿlām al-Nubalā'* (10/656-658).

49 The Egyptian scholar and jurist, Ashhab ibn ʿAbd al-ʿAzīz. It is said that his name was Miskīn and that "Ashhab" was a nickname of his. He was born in 140 AH and died in 204 AH. His biography can be found in *Siyar Aʿlām al-Nubalā'* (9/500-503).

50 This would be legislating without a transmission [from the Prophet s] to rely on. Shāfiʿī differed, saying: "I do not dislike, after Allah has been named at the time of slaughtering animals, for 'May Allah Exalted send His Blessings and Salutations upon him'. Rather, I advocate that."

51 Reported by Nasā'ī (3/91-92), Abū Dāwūd (1047), and Ibn Mājah (1085).

Another time blessings should be sent is when entering the mosque.

Abū Isḥāq ibn Shaʿbān said: "It is befitting for the person who enters the mosque to send blessings upon the Prophet ﷺ and upon his family, ask for mercy for him and his family, seek bounties for him and his family, send salutations [upon him and his family], and say: 'O Allah, forgive my sins and open the gates of Your Mercy to me.' When they leave, they should say the same, replacing 'Your Mercy' with 'Your Grace.'"[52]

ʿAmr ibn Dīnār[53] said, regarding the statement of Allah Exalted, "When you enter houses, greet one another"[54]: "If no-one is in the house, then say: 'May peace be upon the Prophet, and the Mercy and Blessings of Allah. May peace be upon us and upon the righteous servants of Allah. May peace be upon the People of the House, and the Mercy and Blessings of Allah.'"

Ibn ʿAbbās explained: "The meaning of 'houses' here is mosques."

Al-Nakhaʿī[55] said: "If no-one is in the mosque, then say, 'May peace be upon the Messenger of Allah ﷺ', and if no-one is in the house, then say, 'May peace be upon us and upon the righteous servants of Allah.'"

ʿAlqamah[56] said: "When I enter the mosque, I say: 'May peace be upon you, O Prophet, and the Mercy and Blessings of Allah. May Allah send His Blessings upon Muhammad and His Angels supplicate for him.'" Kaʿb related something for entering and exiting the mosque,

---

Authenticated by Ibn Khuzaymah (1733), Dāraquṭnī, and Nawawī in *Riyāḍ al-Ṣāliḥīn* (1212) with my commentary. Also authenticated by Ḥākim (1/278), and Dhahabī concurred. Its referencing can be found in *Mawārid al-Ẓamʾān* (550).

52 Reported by Tirmidhī (314), Ibn Mājah (771), Aḥmad (6/282), and Ibn al-Sunnī (87) from Fāṭimah in a *marfūʿ* narration.

53 The Shaykh of the Sacred Mosque of his time, ʿAmr ibn Dīnār al-Athram al-Makkī. He was born in 45 or 46 AH and died in 126 AH. His biography can be found in *Siyar Aʿlām al-Nubalāʾ* (5/300-307).

54 *al-Nūr*, 61.

55 The imam, *ḥāfiẓ*, and jurist of Iraq, Ibrāhīm ibn Yazīd al-Nakhaʿī. He passed away in 96 AH, having lived for either forty-nine or fifty-eight years. His biography can be found in *Siyar Aʿlām al-Nubalāʾ* (4/520-529).

56 The jurist, scholar, and reciter of Kufa, ʿAlqamah ibn Qays al-Nakhaʿī. He was born in the time of the Muhammadan Messengership, and he is counted amongst those who lived through both the times of Jāhiliyyah and Islam. He passed away after 60 AH, although others said it was after 70 AH. His biography can be found in *Siyar Aʿlām al-Nubalāʾ* (4/53-61).

but he did not mention the invocation of blessings. Ibn Shaʿbān used the narration of Fāṭimah, the daughter of the Messenger of Allah ﷺ, as evidence, [in which she mentions] that the Prophet ﷺ used to do that when he entered the mosque.[57] The same was related from Abū Bakr ibn ʿAmr ibn Ḥazm[58], who also mentions invoking peace and mercy [upon the Prophet ﷺ].

Another time of sending blessings upon the Prophet ﷺ is during the Funeral Prayer.

It is related from Abū Umāmah[59] as being from the Sunnah.[60]

Another context for sending blessings upon the Prophet ﷺ which the Muslim community has adopted and which there is no problem with is sending blessings upon the Prophet ﷺ and upon his family in written messages after the *basmalah*[61]. This was not practiced in the early period but was initiated during the rule of the Banū Hāshim and from there [spread and] was practiced by people across the world.

The Prophet ﷺ said: "Whoever invokes blessings upon me in writing, the Angels continue seeking forgiveness for them for as long as my name remains in that text."[62]

---

57 Reported by Tirmidhī (314), Ibn Mājah (771), Aḥmad (6/282), and Ibn al-Sunnī (87). Tirmidhī said: "The narration of Fāṭimah is *ḥasan*, but its chain is not connected."

58 The emir and then judge of Madinah, and an upright imam, Abū Bakr ibn Muhammad ibn ʿAmr ibn Ḥazm al-Anṣārī. His name and *kunyah* are the same, although some said that his *kunyah* was Abū Muhammad. He passed away in 120 AH, although some suggested other dates. His biography can be found in *Siyar Aʿlām al-Nubalā'* (5/313-314).

59 Asʿad ibn Sahl ibn Ḥunayf. He is counted as a Companion, and he saw the Prophet ﷺ. He passed away in 100 AH at the age of ninety-two. See *Taqrīb al-Tahdhīb*.

60 Reported by Shāfiʿī in his *Musnad* (581), Bayhaqī (4/40), and others, from the narration of Abū Umāmah where he says that he was informed of this by some of the Companions of the Messenger of Allah ﷺ. Also reported in condensed form by Nasā'ī (4/85) from the narration of Abū Umāmah beginning with: "The Sunnah of the Funeral Prayer is..." Authenticated by Nawawī, Ibn Ḥajar, and others. See *Jāmiʿ al-Uṣūl* (6/219).

61 Translator's note: i.e., "In the Name of Allah – the Most Compassionate, Most Merciful."

62 Related by Ṭabarānī in *Al-Awsaṭ* and by others from Abū Hurayrah. Haythamī said in *Majmaʿ al-Zawā'id* (1/137): "Its chain contains Bishr ibn ʿUbayd al-

Another context for invoking blessings upon the Prophet ﷺ is during the *tashahhud* of prayer.

Abū al-Qāsim Khalaf ibn Ibrāhīm al-Muqri' al-Khaṭīb (The Reciter and Orator) and others narrated from Karīmah bint Aḥmad[63], from Abū al- Haytham, from Muhammad ibn Yūsuf, from Muhammad ibn Ismāʿīl, from Abū Nuʿaym, from al-Aʿmash, from Shaqīq ibn Salamah, from ʿAbdullāh ibn Masʿūd, that the Prophet ﷺ said: "When one of you prays, they should say: 'All salutations belong to Allah, and all blessings and pure things. May peace be upon you, O Prophet, and the Mercy and Blessings of Allah. May peace be upon us and upon the righteous servants of Allah', for if you say that, you will reach every righteous servant in the Heavens and Earth [with your supplication]."[64]

This is one of the contexts for invoking peace upon the Prophet ﷺ and his Sunnah for the first *tashahhud*.

Mālik related from Ibn ʿUmar that he used to say that when he had completed his *tashahhud* and wished to make the *taslīm*.[65] In *Al-Mabsūṭ*,[66] Mālik favoured making the same invocation before the *taslīm*.

Muhammad ibn Maslamah said: "What he meant was what was related from ʿĀ'ishah and Ibn ʿUmar, that they both used to say in their invocations of peace: 'May peace be upon you, O Prophet, and the Mercy and Blessings of Allah. May peace be upon us and upon the righteous servants of Allah. May peace be upon you.'"[67]

Dārisī. Al-Azdī said he is a liar, as did others." Suyūṭī extended its attribution in *Al-Manāhil*, p. 1080, to Abū al-Shaykh in *Al-Thawāb* with a weak chain. Mentioned by Ibn al-Jawzī in *Al-Mawḍūʿāt*. Ibn Kathīr said in his *Tafsīr* (3/516): "This hadith is not authentic. Dhahabī said: 'I think it is fabricated (*mawḍūʿ*).'" See also *Al-Qawl al-Badīʿ*, p. 354.

63 Her biography can be found in *Siyar Aʿlām al-Nubalā'* (18/233-235).

64 Reported here from Bukhārī (831). Also reported by Muslim (402).

65 Reported by Mālik in *Al-Muwaṭṭa'* (1/91) and its chain is *ṣaḥīḥ*. It is a *mawqūf* narration with the ruling of a *marfūʿ* narration, for one does not say something like this based on their own opinion.

66 A book on Mālikī jurisprudence by Ismāʿīl al-Qāḍī.

67 Both the narrations of Ibn ʿUmar and ʿĀ'ishah are reported by Mālik in *Al-Muwaṭṭa'* (1/91). Their chains are *ṣaḥīḥ*, and both are *mawqūf* narrations with the ruling of *marfūʿ* narrations.

The people of knowledge favoured for people to intend every righteous servant in the Heavens and Earth – Angels, humans, and Jinn included – as the subject of their supplication.

Mālik said in *Al-Majmūʿah*[68]: "I consider it recommended for a person being led in prayer to say, after their imam utters the *taslīm*: 'May peace be upon you, O Prophet, and the Mercy and Blessings of Allah. May peace be upon us and upon the righteous servants of Allah. May peace be upon you.'"

HOW BLESSINGS AND SALUTATIONS ARE SENT UPON THE PROPHET ﷺ

I read the following hadith to Abū Isḥāq Ibrāhīm ibn Jaʿfar al-Faqīh, who narrated from Qāḍī Abū al-Aṣbagh, from Abū ʿAbdillāh ibn ʿAttāb, from Abū Bakr ibn Wāfid and others, from Abū ʿĪsā, from ʿUbaydullāh, from Yaḥyā, from Mālik, from ʿAbdullāh ibn Abī Bakr ibn ʿAmr ibn Ḥazm, from his father, from ʿAmr ibn Sulaym al-Zuraqī, who said: "Abū Aḥmad al-Sāʿidī informed me that they asked: 'O Messenger of Allah! How do we send blessings upon you?'

He replied: 'Say: "O Allah, send blessings upon Muhammad, his wives, and his offspring, as You sent blessings upon the family of Ibrāhīm, and send bounties upon Muhammad, his wives, and his offspring, as You sent bounties upon the family of Ibrāhīm. You are Praiseworthy, All-Glorious."'"[69]

In the transmission of Mālik from Abū Masʿūd al-Anṣārī, the Prophet ﷺ said: "Say: 'O Allah, send blessings upon Muhammad and upon his family, as You sent blessings upon the family of Ibrāhīm, and send bounties upon Muhammad and upon his family, as You sent bounties upon the family of Ibrāhīm in the worlds. You are Praiseworthy, All-Glorious', and the invocation of peace is as you have learnt."[70]

And in the transmission of Kaʿb ibn ʿUjrah, he said: "O Allah, send blessings upon Muhammad and upon his family, as You sent blessings

68 Al-Khafājī (3/468) said: "It is said that he is referring to *Al-Mudawwanah*."

69 Reported here from Mālik in *Al-Muwaṭṭa'* (1/165) from the chain of Mālik reported by Bukhārī (3369) and Muslim (407).

70 Reported by Mālik in *Al-Muwaṭṭa'* (1/165-166) from the chain of Mālik reported by Muslim (405).

upon Ibrāhīm, and send bounties upon Muhammad and upon his Family, as You sent bounties upon Ibrāhīm. You are Praiseworthy, All-Glorious."[71]

In the narration of ʿUqbah ibn ʿAmr[72], he said: "O Allah, send blessings upon Muhammad, the unlettered Prophet, and upon the family of Muhammad."[73]

And in the transmission of Abū Saʿīd al-Khudrī, he said, "O Allah, send blessings upon Muhammad, Your servant and Messenger",[74] and mentioned something similar.

I heard the following hadith from Qāḍī Abū ʿAbdillāh al-Tamīmī and read it to Abū ʿAlī al-Ḥasan ibn Ṭarīf al-Naḥwī, who [both] narrated from Abū ʿAbdillāh ibn Saʿdūn al-Faqīh, from Abū Bakr al-Muṭawwaʿī, from Abū ʿAbdillāh al-Ḥākim, from Abū Bakr ibn Abī Dārim al-Ḥāfiẓ, from ʿAlī ibn Aḥmad al-ʿIjlī, from Ḥarb ibn al-Ḥasan, from Yaḥyā ibn al-Musāwir, from ʿAmr ibn Khālid, from Zayd ibn ʿAlī ibn al-Ḥusayn, [from his father ʿAlī, from his father al-Ḥusayn,] from his father ʿAlī ibn Abī Ṭālib, who said: "The Messenger of Allah ﷺ counted them out on my hand, saying: 'Jibrīl counted them out on my hand, saying: "This is how it was revealed from the Lord of Honour. 'O Allah, send blessings upon Muhammad and upon the family of Muhammad, as You sent blessings upon Ibrāhīm and upon the family of Ibrāhīm. You are Praiseworthy, All-Glorious. O Allah, send bounties upon Muhammad and upon the family of Muhammad, as You sent bounties upon Ibrāhīm and upon the family of Ibrāhīm. You are Praiseworthy, All-Glorious. O Allah, have mercy upon Muhammad and upon the family of Muhammad, as You had mercy upon Ibrāhīm and upon the family of Ibrāhīm. You are Praiseworthy, All-Glorious. O Allah, show compassion towards Muhammad and towards the family of Muhammad, as You showed compassion towards Ibrāhīm and towards the family of Ibrāhīm. You are Praiseworthy, All-Glorious. O Allah, send salutations upon Muhammad and upon the family of

---

71 Reported by Bukhārī (6357) and Muslim (406).

72 The veteran of Badr, Abū Masʿūd al-Anṣārī.

73 Reported by Abū Dāwūd (981). The root of the narration is reported by Muslim (405). Translator's note: The phrase "the unlettered Prophet" is added in the transmission of Abū Dāwūd.

74 Reported by Bukhārī (6358).

Muhammad, as You sent salutations upon Ibrāhīm and upon the family of Ibrāhīm. You are Praiseworthy, All-Glorious.'"'"[75]

Abū Hurayrah ﷺ narrates that the Prophet ﷺ said: "Whoever would be pleased to be measured out the fullest measure when they send blessings upon us, the People of the House, should say: 'O Allah, send blessings upon Muhammad the Prophet, his wives the Mothers of the Believers, his children, and the People of his House, as You sent blessings upon Ibrāhīm. You are Praiseworthy, All-Glorious.'"[76]

In the transmission of Khārijah al-Anṣārī, ʿAlī ﷺ said: "I asked the Prophet ﷺ: 'How do we send blessings upon you?'

He replied: 'Send blessings upon us and endeavour in your supplications. Then, say: "O Allah, send bounties upon Muhammad and upon the family of Muhammad, as You sent bounties upon Ibrāhīm. You are Praiseworthy, All-Glorious."'"[77]

Salamah al-Kindī narrates: "ʿAlī ﷺ would teach us the invocation of blessings upon the Prophet ﷺ, saying: 'O Allah, Leveller of Lands and Creator of the Seven Heavens, place Your most exalted Blessings, abundant Bounties, and tender Mercy upon Muhammad, Your slave and Messenger, the one who opens that which has been locked, seals those who preceded, truthfully proclaims the truth, and destroys the armies of falsehood, as he was given the duty of doing. He executed Your Command in obedience to You, rushing to gain Your Pleasure. He is conscious of Your Revelation,[78] preserves Your Covenant, and

---

75 Reported here from *Maʿrifah al-ʿUlūm al-Ḥadīth*, pp. 32-33. It is a *musalsal* narration, with the counting on the hands [being repeated by each narrator]. Also reported by Bayhaqī in *Shuʿab al-Īmān*, Abū Nuʿaym in *Maʿrifah*, Daylamī in his *Musnad*, Ibn Bashkuwāl, Abū Fayḍ al-Fādānī in *Al-ʿUjālah fī al-Aḥādīth al-Musalsalah* (91), and other scholars of *musalsal* narrations. Its chain contains three weak narrators, one of whom had lying and fabrication attributed to them. Ibn Ḥajar said in his *Amālīh*: "I believe the narration is fabricated." ʿIrāqī said: "It is very weak." Suyūṭī commented: "Most of what is said about it is that it is weak."

76 Reported by Abū Dāwūd (982). Its chain contains Ḥibbān ibn Yasār al-Kilābī. Ibn Ḥajar said in *Taqrīb al-Tahdhīb*: "He was a truthful man who would get confused." See also *Al-Qawl al-Badīʿ*, p. 67.

77 Reported by Nasāʾī (3/49), Aḥmad (1/199), and others. Graded sound by Suyūṭī in *Al-Jāmiʿ al-Ṣaghīr* (5033).

78 i.e., he understands and preserves it.

proceeds with fulfilling Your Command until the truth was illuminated to the one seeking it and the Blessings of Allah reached their intended recipients. Through him, hearts were guided after wading through tribulation and sin. He clarified the signs, manifest rulings, and illuminators of Islam. He is Your trusted trustee, treasurer of Your reposited Knowledge, witness on the Day of Reckoning. He is the one You sent as a blessing and Your Messenger with the truth [sent] as mercy. O Allah, grant him ample space in Your Eden[79], grant him with multiplied rewards from Your Favour, filling him with joy and not troubling him, from the attainment of Your unrestricted Reward and the abundance of Your continuous Bounties. O Allah, elevate his constructions above the constructions of the people, honour his resting place and reception with You, complete his light for him, and reward him for Your sending of him with an endorsed testimony, accepted statement (i.e., intercession), [as] one with a just rationale, distinguishing strategy, and magnificent proof.'"[80]

He also narrated, regarding the invocation of blessings upon [mentioned in the verse], "Indeed, Allah showers His Blessings upon the Prophet, and His Angels pray for him. O believers! Invoke the Blessings of Allah upon him, and salute him with worthy greetings of peace",[81]: "At Your service, O Allah, my Lord, and Pleasure. May the Blessings of Allah, the Most Kind, Most Merciful, His close Angels, truthful Prophets, righteous martyrs, and anything that glorifies You, O Lord of all worlds, be upon Muhammad ibn ʿAbdillāh, the seal of the Prophets, leader of the Messengers, imam of the righteous, Messenger of the Lord of all worlds, witness and bearer of good news,

---

79 i.e., Your Eternal Paradise.

80 Reported by Ibn Abī Shaybah, Saʿīd ibn Manṣūr, Ṭabarī, Ṭabarānī, and others. Mentioned by Haythamī in *Majmaʿ al-Zawā'id* (10/163-164), where he said: "It was related by Ṭabarānī in *Al-Awsaṭ*. The narration of Salamah al-Kindī from ʿAlī is *mursal*, and the rest of its narrators are *ṣaḥīḥ*." Ibn Kathīr said in his *Tafsīr* (Sūrah al-Aḥzāb, 3/509): "Its chain is subject to discussion. Our Shaykh Abū al-Ḥajjāj al-Mizzī said: 'This Salamah al-Kindī is not known and he did not meet ʿAlī." Sakhāwī graded its chain weak in *Al-Qawl al-Badīʿ*, p. 69, and Ibn Ḥajar withheld comment on it in *Fatḥ al-Bārī* (11/158).

Further explanation of this narration can be found in *Al-Qawl al-Badīʿ*, p. 145.

81 *al-Aḥzāb*, 56.

caller to You by Your permission, and beacon of light, and may peace be upon him."[82]

And from ʿAbdullāh ibn Masʿūd: "O Allah, place Your blessings, bounties, and mercy upon the Leader of the Messengers, the Imam of the Righteous, the Seal of the Prophets, Muhammad, Your servant and Messenger, the Imam of Good and the Messenger of Mercy. O Allah, raise him at the praiseworthy station that both the early and later generations envy him for. O Allah, send blessings upon Muhammad and upon the family of Muhammad, as You sent blessings upon Ibrāhīm and upon the family of Ibrāhīm. You are Praiseworthy, All-Glorious. And send bounties upon Muhammad and upon the family of Muhammad, as You sent bounties upon Ibrāhīm and upon the family of Ibrāhīm. You are Praiseworthy, All-Glorious."[83]

Al-Ḥasan al-Baṣrī used to say: "Whoever wishes to drink the fullest cup from the Fount of the Chosen One should say: 'O Allah, send blessings upon Muhammad and upon his family, his Companions, his children, his wives, his offspring, the People of his House, his in-laws, his supporters and followers, and his loved ones and community, and upon us with all of them, O Most merciful of the Merciful!'"[84]

Ṭāwūs narrated that Ibn ʿAbbās used to say: "O Allah, accept the great intercession of Muhammad, raise his exalted rank, and grant his request in the earlier [life], as You granted [the requests of] Ibrāhīm and Mūsā."[85]

It is related that Wuhayb ibn al-Ward[86] used to say in his supplications: "O Allah, give Muhammad the best of what he asked

82 Sakhāwī said in *Al-Qawl al-Badīʿ*, p. 70: "We related it from the narration of ʿAlī in *Al-Shifā'*, but I did not find its root."

83 Reported by Ibn Mājah (906) and ʿAbd al-Razzāq (3109) in a *mawqūf* narration from ʿAbdullāh ibn Masʿūd. Būṣīrī says in his *Zawā'id*: "Its narrators are reliable, except that al-Masʿūdī used to get mixed up towards the end of his life." Mundhirī graded its chain *ḥasan* in *Al-Targhīb wa al-Tarhīb* (2/505), as did Sakhāwī in *Al-Qawl al-Badīʿ*, p. 75. Mughlaṭā'ī said: "It is sound."

84 Attributed by Sakhāwī in *Al-Qawl al-Badīʿ*, p. 71, to al-Numayrī.

85 Reported by ʿAbd al-Razzāq (3104) and Ismāʿīl al-Qāḍī in *Faḍl al-Ṣalāh ʿalā al-Nabī* ﷺ (52). Ibn Kathīr said in his *Tafsīr* (3/513), "Its chain is good, strong, and sound", and Sakhāwī followed him in this position in *Al-Qawl al-Badīʿ*, p. 71.

86 A reliable narrator, devout worshipper, and wise man from Makkah; he was a peer of Ibrāhīm ibn Adham. His name was ʿAbd al-Wahhāb, and he then

You for himself, give Muhammad the best of what anyone from Your creation has asked You for, and give Muhammad the best of anything You will be asked for until the Day of Judgement."

It is related that Ibn Mas'ūd used to say: "If you send blessings upon the Prophet ﷺ, then perfect your blessings upon him – for you do not know, perhaps that will be presented to him – and say: 'O Allah, place Your Blessings, Mercy, and Bounties upon the leader of the Messengers, imam of the righteous, seal of the Prophets, Muhammad, Your servant and Messenger, imam of good, commander of good, and Messenger of mercy. O Allah, raise him at the praiseworthy station that both the early and later generations envy him for. O Allah, send blessings upon Muhammad and upon the family of Muhammad, as You sent blessings upon Ibrāhīm and upon the family of Ibrāhīm. You are Praiseworthy, All-Glorious. O Allah, send bounties upon Muhammad and upon the family of Muhammad, as You sent bounties upon Ibrāhīm and upon the family of Ibrāhīm. You are Praiseworthy, All-Glorious."[87]

Many other lengthy formulas for sending blessings upon the Prophet ﷺ and praising his family and others have also been related.

The statement of the Prophet ﷺ, "The invocation of peace is as you have learnt",[88] is the invocation Allah taught them in the *tashahhud*: "May peace be upon you, O Prophet, and the Mercy and Blessings of Allah. May peace be upon us and upon the righteous servants of Allah."

In the *tashahhud* of 'Alī ؓ, [the invocation is as follows]: "May peace be upon the Prophet of Allah, may peace be upon the Prophets and Messengers of Allah, may peace be upon the Messenger of Allah, may peace be upon Muhammad ibn 'Abdillāh, may peace be upon us and upon the male and female believers, both those who are absent and those who are present. O Allah, forgive Muhammad, accept his intercession, forgive the people of his house, forgive me, my parents[89]

---

became known by the diminutive form "Wuhayb". He passed away in Makkah in 153 AH. See *Taqrīb al-Tahdhīb* and *Siyar A'lām al-Nubalā'*.

87 Reported by Ibn Mājah (906) and 'Abd al-Razzāq (3109).

88 Reported by Muslim (405) from Abū Mas'ūd al-Badrī ('Uqbah ibn 'Amr).

89 Sakhāwī said in *Al-Qawl al-Badī'*, p. 102: "'Alī said this part as a means of teaching, not because he was supplicating for his own parents, because it is established in a sound narration that his father died as a disbeliever, as stated by al-Mizzī."

and their children, and have mercy on the two of them[90]. May peace be upon us and upon the righteous servants of Allah. May peace be upon you, O Prophet, and the Mercy and Blessings of Allah."

It is stated in this narration from ʿAlī ﷺ that to supplicate for the Prophet ﷺ is to seek forgiveness for him. In the previous narration of his invocation of blessings upon the Prophet ﷺ, it is explained as seeking mercy for the Prophet ﷺ, but this is not related in any other well-known, *marfūʿ* narration.

Abū ʿUmar ibn ʿAbd al-Barr and others took the view that one should not seek mercy for the Prophet ﷺ, but rather should supplicate for the blessings and bounties specified for him, and to supplicate for mercy and forgiveness for others.[91]

Abū Muhammad ibn Abī Zayd included in his invocation of blessings upon the Prophet ﷺ: "O Allah, have mercy on Muhammad and the family of Muhammad, as You had mercy to Ibrāhīm and the family of Ibrāhīm." This was not related in any sound narration, but his evidence was the statement of the Prophet ﷺ: "May peace be upon you, O Prophet, and the Mercy and Blessings of Allah."

---

90 Translator's note: i.e., the parents.

91 The permissibility of seeking mercy for the Prophet ﷺ is the position of the majority of scholars, as documented by Ibn Kathīr in his *Tafsīr* (Sūrah al-Aḥzāb, 3/509). Nawawī considered making that a recommended action to be an innovation with no [authentic] source. He said in *Al-Adhkār* (notes to hadith no. 360) with my commentary: "As for what some of our companions and Ibn Abī Zayd al-Mālikī say about the desirability of adding to that, 'and have mercy upon Muhammad and the family of Muhammad', this is an innovation with no source." Imam Abū Bakr ibn al-ʿArabī al-Mālikī was emphatic of his censuring of the practice, the mistake of Ibn Abī Zayd al-Mālikī, and the ignorance of the one who adds this phrase in his book *Sharḥ al-Tirmidhī*. He said: "Because the Prophet ﷺ taught us how to send blessings upon him, adding to it is tantamount to saying that his statement is deficient and is being rectified, and [all] success is with Allah."

THE VIRTUE OF SENDING BLESSINGS AND SALUTATIONS UPON THE PROPHET ﷺ AND SUPPLICATING ON HIS BEHALF

The righteous Shaykh Aḥmad ibn Muhammad informed us in his writings that Qāḍī Yūnus ibn Mughīth, from Abū Bakr ibn Muʿāwiyah, from al-Nasāʾī, from Suwayd ibn Naṣr, from ʿAbdullāh, from Ḥaywah ibn Shurayḥ, who said: "Kaʿb ibn ʿAlqamah informed me that he heard ʿAbdullāh ibn Jubayr, the servant of Nāfiʿ, [stating] that he heard ʿAbdullāh ibn ʿAmr say: 'I heard the Messenger of Allah ﷺ say: "When you hear the muezzin, repeat what he says and [then] invoke blessings upon me, for whoever invokes one blessing upon me, Allah sends ten blessings upon them. Then, ask Allah to grant me the close position (*al-wasīlah*), for it is a station in Paradise that is suitable for only one of the slaves of Allah and I hope that I am that slave. Whoever asks for the close position on my behalf will be granted intercession."'"[92]

Anas ibn Mālik narrated that the Prophet ﷺ said: "Whoever invokes a blessing upon me, Allah sends ten blessings upon them, removes ten of their transgressions, and raises them ten degrees [in rank]."[93]

And in another transmission: "...and writes ten good deeds for them."[94]

Anas also narrated that the Prophet ﷺ said: "Jibrīl called me, saying: 'Whoever invokes a blessing upon you, Allah sends ten blessings upon them and raises them ten degrees [in rank].'"[95]

And in the transmission of ʿAbd al-Raḥmān ibn ʿAwf, the Prophet ﷺ said: "I met Jibrīl and he said to me: 'I give you the good news that Allah Exalted says: "Whoever invokes salutations upon you, I send

---

92 Reported here from Nasāʾī (2/25). Also reported by Muslim (384).

93 Reported by Nasāʾī (3/50) and others. Authenticated by Ibn Ḥibbān in *Mawārid al-Ẓamʾān* (2390). Also authenticated by Ḥākim (1/550), and Dhahabī concurred. Ibn Ḥajar said: "Its narrators are reliable." Its referencing can be found in *Mawārid al-Ẓamʾān*.

94 Reported by Aḥmad (2/262) from Abū Hurayrah. Haythamī said in *Majmaʿ al-Zawāʾid* (10/160): "Its narrators are *ṣaḥīḥ* except Ribʿiyy ibn Ibrāhīm, who is trusted and reliable." See also Tirmidhī (484) and *Majmaʿ al-Zawāʾid* (10/161-162).

95 Reported by Bazzār (3159) and others. Haythamī said in *Majmaʿ al-Zawāʾid* (10/161): "Its chain contains Salamah ibn Wardān, who is a weak narrator." See also *Al-Qawl al-Badīʿ*, p. 158.

salutations upon them, and whoever invokes blessings upon you, I send blessings upon them.'""[96]

Similar was reported from Abū Hurayrah,[97] Mālik ibn Aws ibn al-Ḥadathān,[98] ʿUbaydullāh,[99] and Ibn Abī Ṭalḥah.[100]

Zayd ibn al-Ḥubāb[101] narrated: "I heard the Prophet ﷺ say: 'Whoever says, "O Allah, send blessings upon Muhammad and grant him the near station by You on the Day of Judgement", my intercession is mandated for them.'"[102]

Ibn Masʿūd narrated that the Prophet ﷺ said: "The people most deserving of me on the Day of Judgement will be those who invoked the most blessings upon me."[103]

---

96 Reported by Aḥmad (1/191) and Ismāʿīl al-Qāḍī in *Faḍl al-Ṣalāh ʿalā al-Nabī* ﷺ (7). Authenticated by Ḥākim (1/550), and Dhahabī concurred. Haythamī said in *Majmaʿ al-Zawāʾid* (2/287): "Its narrators are reliable."

97 Reported by Muslim (408).

98 Reported by Bukhārī in *Al-Adab al-Mufrad* (642). Its chain contains Salamah ibn Wardān, who was said in *Taqrīb al-Tahdhīb* to be a weak narrator, but the hadith is strengthened by other supporting evidence.

99 ʿAbdullāh ibn Abī Ṭalḥah al-Anṣārī. His mother was Umm Sulaym, the mother of Anas ibn Mālik, and his father was Abū Ṭalḥah al-Anṣārī (Zayd ibn Sahl). Ibn Ḥajar said: "He passed away in Madinah in 84 AH."

100 Reported by Nasāʾī (3/44, 50) and others from ʿAbdullāh ibn Abī Ṭalḥah al-Anṣārī from his father. Authenticated by Ibn Ḥibbān in *Mawārid al-Ẓamʾān* (2391) and Suyūṭī in *Al-Manāhil*, p. 1083. Also authenticated by Ḥākim (2/420-421), and Dhahabī concurred. Its referencing can be found in *Mawārid al-Ẓamʾān*.

101 This should actually say "Ruwayfiʿ ibn Thābit al-Anṣārī narrated: 'I heard the Prophet ﷺ say'", because he is the Companion who narrated this hadith, as is clarified in its referencing. Zayd ibn Ḥubāb is one of the narrators in its chain. He was from the ninth generation, and he died in 203 AH. Sakhāwī identifies this mistake in *Al-Qawl al-Badīʿ*, p. 66.

102 Reported by Bazzār (3157), Ṭabarānī in *Al-Kabīr* and *Al-Awsaṭ* and elsewhere from Ruwayfiʿ ibn Thābit al-Anṣārī. Mundhirī said in *Al-Targhīb wa al-Tarhīb* (2/504): "Some of their chains are *ḥasan*." Haythamī said in *Majmaʿ al-Zawāʾid* (1/163): "Their chains are *ḥasan*." Also reported by Aḥmad (4/108). Ibn Kathīr said in his *Tafsīr* (3/513): "There is no problem with this chain."

103 Reported by Tirmidhī (484). Authenticated by Ibn Ḥibbān in *Mawārid al-Ẓamʾān* (2389) and graded sound by Suyūṭī in *Al-Jāmiʿ al-Ṣaghīr* (2249). Tirmidhī said: "This hadith is *ḥasan gharīb*", and Baghawī followed him in this view. Its referencing can be found in *Mawārid al-Ẓamʾān*.

And Abū Hurayrah narrated that he said: "Whoever invokes blessings upon me in writing, the Angels continue seeking forgiveness for them for as long as my name remains in that text."[104]

ʿĀmir ibn Rabīʿah narrated: "I heard the Prophet ﷺ say: 'Whoever invokes blessings upon me, the Angels will supplicate for them as much as they invoke blessings. So, a servant may do that a little or a lot.'"[105]

Ubayy ibn Kaʿb narrated: "Whenever a quarter of the night had passed, the Messenger of Allah ﷺ would get up and say: 'O people, remember Allah! The quaking Blast is coming, followed by a second Blast. Death is coming with everything it entails.'"

Ubayy ibn Kaʿb said: "O Messenger of Allah, I am prolific in sending blessings upon you. How much of my supplications should I dedicate to you?"

"As much as you wish", the Prophet ﷺ replied.

"A quarter?" Ubayy asked.

"As much as you wish, and if you increased on that, it would be better for you", the Prophet ﷺ replied.

"A third?" Ubayy asked.

"As much as you wish, and if you increased on that, it would be better for you", the Prophet ﷺ replied.

"A half?" Ubayy asked.

"As much as you wish, and if you increased on that, it would be better for you", the Prophet ﷺ replied.

"Two-thirds?" Ubayy asked.

"As much as you wish, and if you increased on that, it would be better for you", the Prophet ﷺ replied.

"O Messenger of Allah, should I dedicate all my supplications to you?" Ubayy asked.

---

104 Related by Ṭabarānī in *Al-Awsaṭ* and others. Haythamī said in *Majmaʿ al-Zawā'id* (1/137): "Its chain contains Bishr ibn ʿUbayd al-Dārisī. Al-Azdī said he is a liar, as did others."

105 Reported by Ibn Mājah (907), Aḥmad (3/445), and ʿAbd al-Razzāq (3115). Suyūṭī graded its chain *ḥasan* in *Al-Manāhil*, p. 1081. Also graded *ḥasan* by Ibn Ḥajar, as found in *Al-Qawl al-Badīʿ*, p. 169. Būṣīrī said in *Miṣbāḥ al-Zujājah*: "Its chain is weak because Bukhārī and others said the narrations of ʿĀṣim ibn ʿUbaydillāh are odd (*munkar*)."

"In that case, you would be sufficed and your sins would be forgiven", the Prophet ﷺ replied.[106]

Abū Ṭalḥah narrated: "I visited the Prophet ﷺ, and I saw him expressing a cheerfulness and ease I had never seen on him before. I asked him [about that], and he said: 'And what is preventing me [from being joyful] when Jibrīl has just left after coming to me with glad tidings from my Lord ﷻ, saying: "Allah has sent me to you to give you the good news that anyone from your nation who invokes one blessing upon you, Allah will send ten blessings upon them, and His Angels will supplicate for them ten times."'"[107]

Jābir ibn ʿAbdillāh ﷺ narrated: "The Messenger of Allah ﷺ said: 'Whoever says, after hearing the call [to prayer], "O Allah, Lord of this perfect call and established prayer, give Muhammad the close position (*al-wasīlah*) and the superior rank (*al-faḍīlah*), and raise him to the honoured station You promised him", will be granted my intercession on the Day of Judgement.'"[108]

Saʿd ibn Abī Waqqāṣ ﷺ narrates [that the Prophet ﷺ said]: "Whoever says, after hearing the muezzin, 'I bear witness that there is no deity [worthy of worship] except Allah, and that Muhammad is His slave and Messenger. I am pleased with Allah as my Lord, Muhammad as my Messenger, and Islam as my religion', will have their sins forgiven."[109]

Ibn Wahb related that the Prophet ﷺ said: "Whoever sends ten salutations upon me, it is as if they have freed a slave."[110]

In some narrations, he said: "People will come to me whom I do not recognize except by the abundance of the blessings they invoked upon me."[111]

---

106 Reported by Tirmidhī (2457) and others. Authenticated by Ḥākim (2/421), and Dhahabī concurred. Also graded *ḥasan* by Ibn Ḥajar in *Fatḥ al-Bārī* (11/168). Tirmidhī said: "This hadith is *ḥasan ṣaḥīḥ*."

107 Reported by Nasāʾī (3/44, 50) and others.

108 Reported by Bukhārī (614).

109 Reported by Muslim (386).

110 Related by Suyūṭī in *Al-Manāhil*, p. 1085, without its reference. Also found in *Al-Qawl al-Badīʿ*, p. 102.

111 Sakhāwī said in *Al-Qawl al-Badīʿ*, p. 182: "I did not find its chain."

And in others: "The first of you to be rescued on the Day of Judgement from its horrors and stations will be those of you who invoked the most blessings upon me."[112]

Abū Bakr ؓ said: "Invoking blessings upon the Prophet ﷺ is more efficient in effacing sins than cool water to fire, and sending salutations upon him is more virtuous than freeing slaves."[113]

THE DISCREDIBILITY AND SIN OF THE PERSON WHO DOES NOT SEND BLESSINGS UPON THE PROPHET ﷺ

Qāḍī Abū ʿAlī ؓ narrated to us from Abū al-Faḍl ibn Khayrūn and Abū al-Ḥusayn al-Ṣayrafī, who both said: "Abū Yaʿlā and al-Sinjī narrated to us from Muḥammad ibn Maḥbūb, from Abū ʿĪsā, from Aḥmad ibn Ibrāhīm al-Dawraqī, from Ribʿiyy ibn Ibrāhīm, from ʿAbd al-Raḥmān ibn Isḥāq, from Saʿīd ibn Abī Saʿīd, from Abū Hurayrah, who said: 'The Messenger of Allah ﷺ said: "May his nose be rubbed in dust,[114] a man in whose presence I am mentioned and does not send blessings upon me. May his nose be rubbed in dust, a man for whom Ramadan enters and then passes before he has been forgiven. And may his nose be rubbed in dust, a man whose parents reach old age, but he does not enter Paradise on their account."'"

ʿAbd al-Raḥmān commented: "And I think he said: '...or one of his parents.'"[115]

In another narration, [it is related] that the Prophet ﷺ ascended the pulpit and said "*Āmīn*". Then, he ascended again and said "*Āmīn*". Then, he ascended again and said "*Āmīn*". Muʿādh ibn Jabal asked him about that. The Prophet ﷺ answered: "Jibrīl ؑ came to me and said: 'O Muhammad, if you are mentioned in front of someone and they do not send blessings upon you and then they die, they will enter the Fire and Allah will distance them. Say "*Āmīn*"'. So, I said '*Āmīn*'."

Jibrīl ؑ said the same regarding a person who meets Ramadan but does not have it accepted from him, as well as for a person whose

---

112 Related by al-Aṣbahānī in his *Targhīb* from Anas. See *Al-Manāhil*, p. 1087.
113 Related by al-Numayrī, Ibn Bashkuwāl, Ibn ʿAsākir, and others. Sakhāwī said in *Al-Qawl al-Badīʿ*, p. 177: "Its chain is weak."
114 Meaning: "May he be humiliated."
115 Reported here from Tirmidhī (3545). He said: "This hadith is *ḥasan gharīb*."

parents, or one of them, meet old age, but he does not honour them and then dies.[116]

ʿAlī ﵁ narrated that the Prophet ﷺ said: "The stingy one is the person in whose presence I am mentioned and does not send blessings upon me."[117]

Jaʿfar ibn Muhammad narrated from his father: "The Messenger of Allah ﷺ said: 'For a person to have me mentioned in their presence and not send blessings upon me is to err from the path to Paradise.'"[118]

Abū Hurayrah ﵁ narrated: "The Messenger of Allah ﷺ said: 'Any people who sit at an assembly and then depart before remembering Allah or invoking blessings upon the Prophet ﷺ, will bear a liability before Allah. If He wishes, He will punish them, and if He wishes, He will forgive them.'"[119]

Abū Hurayrah ﵁ also narrated that he said: "Whoever neglects sending blessings upon me neglects the path to Paradise."[120]

---

116 This hadith was related from several Companions. Ibn al-Qayyim said in *Jalā' al-Afhām*, p. 383: "Undoubtedly, a narration having these supporting chains signifies authenticity." Taken here from *Mawārid al-Ẓam'ān* (2028), where it is reported from Abū Hurayrah.

117 Mentioned by Ibn Ḥajar in *Fatḥ al-Bārī* (11/167-168), where he said: "Reported by Tirmidhī, Nasā'ī, Ibn Ḥibbān, Ḥākim, and Ismāʿīl al-Qāḍī, expanding on its chains and clarifying the differences of opinion about the narration, from ʿAlī, from his son al-Ḥusayn, and it does not fall below the grade of *ḥasan*." The narration of al-Ḥusayn ibn ʿAlī is taken here from *Mawārid al-Ẓam'ān* (2388).

118 Reported by Bayhaqī in *Shuʿab al-Īmān* in a *mursal* narration. Munāwī said in *Fayḍ al-Qadīr* (6/129): "Qasṭallānī said: 'A *maʿlūl* hadith.'" Attributed by Ibn Ḥajar in *Fatḥ al-Bārī* (11/168) to Ibn Mājah (908) from Ibn ʿAbbās, Bayhaqī in *Shuʿab al-Īmān* from Abū Hurayrah, Ibn Abī Ḥātim from Jābir, and Ṭabarānī from al-Ḥusayn ibn ʿAlī. Ibn Ḥajar said: "These chains support each other." See *Al-Qawl al-Badīʿ*, pp. 213-215, and *Majmaʿ al-Zawā'id* (10/164).

119 Reported by Tirmidhī (3380), Aḥmad (2/446), and others. Authenticated by Ḥākim (1/550), and Dhahabī concurred. Graded sound by Suyūṭī in *Al-Jāmiʿ al-Ṣaghīr* (2982). Tirmidhī said: "This hadith is *ḥasan ṣaḥīḥ*." Its referencing can be found in *Mawārid al-Ẓam'ān* (2321, 2322).

120 Reported by Bayhaqī in *Shuʿab al-Īmān* and *Al-Sunan al-Kubrā* and by others. Al-Rashīd al-ʿAṭṭār graded its chain sound, as found in *Al-Qawl al-Badīʿ*, p. 214.

Qatādah narrated that the Prophet said: "Part of harshness is for me to be mentioned in the presence of a man and he to not send blessings upon me."[121]

Jābir narrated that he said: "Any people who sit at an assembly and then depart without invoking blessings upon the Prophet, depart with a stench fouler than a corpse."[122]

Abū Saʿīd narrated that the Prophet said: "Any people who sit at an assembly in which they do not invoke blessings upon the Prophet, will suffer regret, and if they enter Paradise, they will not see the reward [of doing so]."[123]

Tirmidhī related from some of the people of knowledge: "For a man to invoke blessings upon the Prophet once during a gathering will suffice him for the whole gathering."[124]

THE DISTINCTION OF THE PROPHET IN HAVING ANY CREATURE'S INVOCATION OF BLESSINGS UPON HIM CONVEYED TO HIM

Qāḍī Abū ʿAbdillāh al-Tamīmī[125] narrated to us from al-Ḥusayn ibn Muhammad, from Abū ʿAmr al-Ḥāfiẓ, from Ibn ʿAbd al-Mu'min, from Ibn Dāsah, from Abū Dāwūd, from Ibn ʿAwf, from al-Muqri', from Ḥaywah, from Abū Ṣakhr Ḥumayd ibn Ziyād, from Yazīd ibn ʿAbdillāh ibn Qusayṭ, from Abū Hurayrah, that the Messenger of Allah said:

---

121 A *mursal* narration. Reported by ʿAbd al-Razzāq in his *Jāmiʿ*, as found in *Fatḥ al-Bārī* (11/168) and *Al-Qawl al-Badīʿ*, p. 215. Sakhāwī said: "Its narrators are reliable." Graded weak by Suyūṭī in *Al-Jāmiʿ al-Ṣaghīr* (8215). Also reported by ʿAbd al-Razzāq in *Al-Muṣannaf* in a *mursal* narration from Muhammad ibn ʿAlī.

122 Reported by Nasā'ī in *ʿAmal al-Yawm wa al-Laylah* (58, 411) and by others. Authenticated by al-Ḍiyā' in *Al-Mukhtārah*. Sakhāwī said in *Al-Qawl al-Badīʿ*, p. 222: "Its narrators are *ṣaḥīḥ* according to the conditions of Muslim."

123 Reported by Tirmidhī in the comments to (3380) from Abū Hurayrah and Abu Saʿīd al-Khudrī. Graded *ḥasan* by Suyūṭī in *Al-Jāmiʿ al-Ṣaghīr* (7886). Reported by Nasā'ī in *ʿAmal al-Yawm wa al-Laylah* (410) in a *mawqūf* narration from Abu Saʿīd.

124 Reported by Tirmidhī in the comments to (3545).

125 His biography can be found in *Siyar Aʿlām al-Nubalā'* (19/266).

"[For] any person who sends salutations upon me, Allah returns my soul so that I may return the salutations to them."[126]

Abū Bakr ibn Abī Shaybah mentioned that Abū Hurayrah ﵁ narrated: "The Messenger of Allah ﷺ said: 'I hear whoever sends blessings upon me at my grave, and I am informed of whoever sends blessings upon me from a distance.'"[127]

Ibn Masʿūd ﵁ narrated that he said: "Allah has Angels who roam through the land, conveying to me the salutations of my nation."[128] Similar is related from Abū Hurayrah ﵁.[129]

---

126 Reported here from Abū Dāwūd (2041). Also reported by Aḥmad (2/527) and Bayhaqī in *Al-Sunan al-Kubrā* (5/245). Nawawī authenticated its chain in *Al-Adhkār* (356) and *Riyāḍ al-Ṣāliḥīn* (1462) with my commentary. Ibn Ḥajar said, "Its narrators are reliable", and graded its chain *ḥasan* in *Takhrīj al-Adhkār*, and he was followed in that opinion by Suyūṭī in *Al-Manāhil*, p. 1098.

127 Reported by Abū al-Shaykh in *Al-Thawāb* and Bayhaqī in *Shuʿab al-Īmān*. See *Al-Manāhil*, p. 1099. Graded weak by Suyūṭī in *Al-Jāmiʿ al-Ṣaghīr* (8812). Munāwī said in *Fayḍ al-Qadīr* (6/170): "Ibn Ḥajar said in *Fatḥ al-Bārī*, 'Its chain is good (*jayyid*)', but it is not *jayyid*." Sakhāwī said in *Al-Qawl al-Badīʿ*, p. 227: "Its chain is *jayyid*, as our Shaykh has indicated." ʿUqaylī said: "A hadith with no origin." Ibn Daḥiyyah said: "[It is] fabricated." Mentioned by Ibn al-Jawzī in *Al-Mawḍūʿāt*. Ibn Kathīr said in his *Tafsīr* (Sūrah al-Aḥzāb, 3/515): "Its chain is subject to discussion. It was related only by Muhammad ibn Marwān al-Suddī al-Ṣaghīr, and he is not taken from (*matrūk*). Shaykh al-Islām Ibn Taymiyyah gave two different rulings regarding this narration. He said in *Al-Fatāwā* (27/241) that it is fabricated, but he also said in *Al-Fatāwā* (27/116): "Its chain has some weakness, but it has reliable supporting proofs." Ibn al-Qayyim said: "It is *gharīb*."

128 Reported by Nasāʾī (3/43) and others in a *marfūʿ* narration from ʿAbdullāh ibn Masʿūd. Authenticated by Ḥākim (2/421), and Dhahabī concurred. Also authenticated by Ibn Ḥibbān in *Mawārid al-Ẓamʾān* (2392), where its referencing can be found.

129 Reported by Abū Dāwūd (2042), Aḥmad (2/367), and others. Nawawī authenticated its chain in *Riyāḍ al-Ṣāliḥīn* (1461) with my commentary. Ibn Ḥajar said in *Takhrīj al-Adhkār*: "A *ḥasan* hadith." The wording of Abū Dāwūd includes: "Do not make your homes graves, do not make my grave a gathering place (*ʿīd*), and invoke blessings upon me, for your invocations of blessings reach me wherever you are."

Ibn ʿUmar said: "Increase in sending salutations upon your Prophet on Fridays, for they are brought to him from you every Friday."[130]

In another transmission, [the Prophet said]: "...for any time one of you invokes blessings upon me, their invocation of blessings is presented to me when they finish."[131]

Al-Ḥasan ibn ʿAlī narrated that the Prophet said: "Wherever you are, invoke blessings upon me, for your invocations of blessings are conveyed to me."[132]

Ibn ʿAbbās said: "Any person from the nation of Muhammad who sends salutations or blessings upon him, he will be informed of it."[133]

Some mentioned that for any servant [of Allah] who sends blessings upon the Prophet, their name is presented to him.[134]

Al-Ḥasan ibn ʿAlī narrated: "When you enter the mosque, send salutations upon the Prophet, for the Messenger of Allah said: 'Do not take my house as a gathering place (ʿīd),[135] do not take your houses as graves,[136] and invoke blessings upon me wherever you are, for your invocations of blessings are conveyed to me wherever you are.'"[137]

---

130 Mentioned by Sakhāwī in *Al-Qawl al-Badīʿ*, p. 234, where he said: "Mentioned by ʿIyāḍ, and I did not find its chain."

131 Reported by Ibn Mājah (1637) from Abū al-Dardāʾ. Būṣīrī says in his *Zawāʾid*: "This narration is sound, except that it is disconnected in two places." Graded *ḥasan* by Suyūṭī in *Al-Jāmiʿ al-Ṣaghīr* (1403).

132 Reported by Ṭabarānī in *Al-Kabīr* and *Al-Awsaṭ*. Haythamī said in *Majmaʿ al-Zawāʾid* (10/162): "Its chain contains Ḥumayd ibn Abī Zaynab, who I do not recognize, and the rest of its narrators are *ṣaḥīḥ*." It is a *ḥasan* narration, graded *ḥasan* by Mundhirī in *Al-Targhīb wa al-Tarhīb* (2/498), Ibn Ḥajar in *Takhrīj al-Adhkār*, and Sakhāwī in *Al-Qawl al-Badīʿ*, p. 226.

133 Reported by Bayhaqī in *Shuʿab al-Īmān* and Ibn Rāhawayh in his *Musnad*. See *Al-Manāhil*, p. 1104.

134 This is found in a *marfūʿ* narration related by Bazzār, Abū al-Shaykh, and Ṭabarānī from ʿAmmār ibn Yāsir, as found in *Al-Targhīb wa al-Tarhīb* (2/499). Mundhirī said: "They all related it from Nuʿaym ibn Ḍamḍam, who there is a difference of opinion about, from ʿImrān al-Ḥumayrī, who is unknown."

135 i.e., do not make my grave resemble a festival. See *Fayḍ al-Qadīr* (4/199).

136 i.e., do not make them devoid of prayer. See *Fayḍ al-Qadīr* (4/199).

137 Reported by Abū Yaʿlā (6761). Authenticated by al-Ḍiyāʾ in *Al-Mukhtārah* and Suyūṭī in *Al-Jāmiʿ al-Ṣaghīr* (5016). Haythamī said in *Majmaʿ al-Zawāʾid* (2/247): "Its chain contains ʿAbdullāh ibn Nāfiʿ, who is a weak narrator."

And in the narration of Aws, [the Prophet ﷺ said]: "Increase in invoking blessings upon me on Fridays, for your invocations of blessings are presented to me."¹³⁸

Sulaymān ibn Suḥaym narrated: "I saw the Prophet ﷺ in a dream. I asked: 'O Messenger of Allah! These people who come to you and greet you, do you comprehend their greetings?'

'Yes,' he replied, 'and I return them.'"¹³⁹

Ibn Shihāb narrated: "It reached us that the Messenger of Allah ﷺ said: 'Increase in invoking blessings upon me on luminous nights and bright days, for they will be conveyed from you. The earth does not consume the bodies of the Prophets. For every Muslim who invokes blessings upon me, an Angel carries their blessings, conveys them to me, and names them, saying: "So-and-so said such-and-such."'"¹⁴⁰

THE DIFFERENCE OF OPINION REGARDING SENDING BLESSINGS UPON OTHER THAN THE MESSENGER OF ALLAH ﷺ AND THE REST OF THE PROPHETS ﷺ

The majority of scholars agree that it is permissible to invoke blessings upon other than the Prophet ﷺ.

It was related that Ibn ʿAbbās ؓ said: "It is not permissible to invoke blessings upon other than the Prophet ﷺ."¹⁴¹

And: "It is not befitting to invoke blessings upon anyone except Prophets."¹⁴²

---

138 Reported by Nasāʾī (3/91-92), Abū Dāwūd (1047), and Ibn Mājah (1085).

139 Related by Ibn Abī al-Dunyā and by Bayhaqī in *Ḥilyah al-Awliyāʾ* and *Shuʿab al-Īmān*, as stated by Sakhāwī in *Al-Qawl al-Badīʿ*, p. 236.

140 A *mursal* narration. Reported by al-Numayrī, as found in *Al-Qawl al-Badīʿ*, p. 235, and reported in condensed form by Ṭabarānī in *Al-Awsaṭ* and Bayhaqī in *Shuʿab al-Īmān* from Abū Hurayrah. Haythamī said in *Majmaʿ al-Zawāʾid* (2/169): "Its chain contains ʿAbd al-Munʿim ibn Bashīr al-Anṣārī, who is a weak narrator." Sakhāwī said in *Al-Qawl al-Badīʿ*, p. 227: "However, it is strengthened by its supporting evidences." Graded *ḥasan* by Suyūṭī in *Al-Jāmiʿ al-Ṣaghīr* (1402), where he attributed the narration to Ibn ʿAdiyy from Anas, Saʿīd ibn Manṣūr in his *Sunan* from al-Ḥasan, and Khālid ibn Maʿdān in a *mursal* narration. See *Al-Maqāṣid al-Ḥasanah* (148).

141 Reported by Bayhaqī in *Shuʿab al-Īmān* and Saʿīd ibn Manṣūr in his *Sunan*. See *Al-Manāhil*, p. 1108.

142 Reported by ʿAbd al-Razzāq (3119) and Ṭabarānī. Haythamī said in *Majmaʿ*

Sufyān said: "It is disliked to invoke blessings except upon the Prophet ﷺ."[143]

I found in the writings of one of my teachers: "The school of thought (*madhhab*) of Mālik was that it is not permissible to invoke blessings upon any of the Prophets except Muhammad ﷺ." However, this is not generally recognized as the position of his *madhhab*. Mālik said in *Al-Mabsūṭah* to Yaḥyā ibn Isḥāq: "I dislike for blessings to be invoked upon other than Prophets, and it is not appropriate for us to exceed beyond what we have been commanded to do."[144]

Yaḥyā ibn Yaḥyā[145] said: "I do not follow his opinion, and there is no problem with invoking blessings upon any of the Prophets or upon other than them." He used the narration of Ibn ʿUmar ؓ as evidence,[146] as well as the narrations where the Prophet ﷺ was teaching how to send blessings upon him and said: "…and upon his family, and upon his wives."[147]

I found a supplementary note from Abū ʿImrān al-Fāsī[148] in which it is related that Ibn ʿAbbās ؓ disliked for blessings to be invoked upon other than the Prophet ﷺ, saying: "This is the view we follow, and it is not something that was done in the past."

ʿAbd al-Razzāq related that Abū Hurayrah ؓ said: "The Messenger of Allah ﷺ said: 'Send blessings upon the Prophets of Allah and His Messengers, for He sent them as He sent me.'"[149]

---

al-Zawāʾid (10/167): "Related by Ṭabarānī in a *mawqūf* hadith, and its narrators are *ṣaḥīḥ*." Attributed by Ibn Ḥajar in *Fatḥ al-Bārī* (11/169-170) to Ibn Abī Shaybah, and he graded its chain sound.

143 Mentioned by ʿAbd al-Razzāq in *Al-Muṣannaf* (3119).

144 Related by Ibn Ḥajar, from the present author, in *Fatḥ al-Bārī* (11/170).

145 Yaḥyā ibn Yaḥyā ibn Kathīr al-Laythī, the jurist of Andalusia and one of the narrators of *Al-Muwaṭṭaʾ* from Imam Mālik. He was born in 152 AH and died in 233 or 234 AH. His biography can be found in *Siyar Aʿlām al-Nubalāʾ* (10/519-525).

146 The narration of Ibn ʿUmar was reported by Mālik in *Al-Muwaṭṭaʾ* (1/166) and its chain is *ṣaḥīḥ*.

147 As previously related.

148 The great imam and esteemed scholar of al-Qayruwān, Mūsā ibn ʿĪsā al-Mālikī. He was born in 368 AH and passed away in 430 AH. His biography can be found in *Siyar Aʿlām al-Nubalāʾ* (17/545-548).

149 Reported by ʿAbd al-Razzāq in *Al-Muṣannaf* (3118), Ismāʿīl al-Qāḍī, and others. Its chain was graded weak by Ibn Kathīr in his *Tafsīr* (Sūrah al-Aḥzāb, 3/516),

They[150] said that the chains of [the narrations related from] Ibn ʿAbbās are weak. In the Arabic language, "invoking blessings" refers to seeking mercy and supplicating. This applies universally unless there is a sound narration of consensus of opinion to restrict its meaning.

Allah Exalted said: "He is the One Who showers His blessings upon you – and His Angels pray for you – so that He may bring you out of darkness and into light. For He is ever Merciful to the believers."[151]

"Take from their wealth [O Prophet] charity to purify and bless them, and pray for them – surely your prayer is a source of comfort for them. And Allah is All-Hearing, All-Knowing."[152]

And: "They are the ones who will receive blessings and mercy from their Lord."[153]

The Prophet ﷺ said: "O Allah, send blessings upon the family of Abū Awfā." And when people brought their charity to him, he would say: "O Allah, send blessings upon the family of So-and-so."[154]

In the narration describing how to invoke blessings upon him, the Prophet ﷺ said: "O Allah, send blessings upon Muhammad, and upon his wives and offspring."[155]

And in another narration: "...and upon the family of Muhammad."[156] "*Āl*", translated here as "family", has been interpreted as his followers; the people of his house; his nation; his followers, tribe, and clan; his people; his children; and those who are not allowed to consume from *zakāh*.[157]

Ibn Ḥajar in *Fatḥ al-Bārī* (11/169), and Suyūṭī in *Al-Manāhil*, p. 1110. Sakhāwī said in *Al-Qawl al-Badīʿ*, p. 80: "Its chain contains Mūsā ibn ʿUbaydah. Although he is weak, his narrations can be used as secondary evidence."

150 Translator's note: According to Mullā al-Qārī, this refers to Yaḥyā ibn Yaḥyā and his followers, or the majority of scholars.

151 *al-Aḥzāb*, 43.

152 *al-Tawbah*, 103.

153 *al-Baqarah*, 157.

154 Reported by Bukhārī (1497) and Muslim (1078) from ʿAbdullāh ibn Abī Awfā. The wording here is from Bukhārī.

155 Reported by Mālik in *Al-Muwaṭṭa'* (1/165) from the chain of Mālik reported by Bukhārī (3369) and Muslim (407).

156 As previously related.

157 Translator's note: Regarding the final category, see Bukhārī (3072) and Muslim (1072).

In the narration of Anas, [we find]: "The Prophet ﷺ was asked: 'Who are the family of Muhammad?'

He replied: 'Every righteous person.'"[158]

According to the school of thought of al-Ḥasan al-Baṣrī, the intended meaning of "the āl of Muhammad" is the Prophet Muhammad ﷺ himself, for the Prophet ﷺ used to say in invoking blessings upon himself, "O Allah! Place Your blessings and bounties upon the āl of Muhammad", meaning himself. He would not leave an obligatory deed in favour of a supererogatory deed, and the action that Allah Exalted commanded is invoking blessings upon the Prophet Muhammad ﷺ himself.

This is like the statement of the Prophet ﷺ, "I was given one of the flutes from the flutes of the family of Dāwūd", meaning, "from the flutes of Dāwūd". [159]

And in the narration of Abū Ḥumayd al-Sāʿidī on invoking blessings, [the Prophet ﷺ said]: "O Allah, send blessings upon Muhammad, his wives, and his offspring."[160]

Ibn ʿUmar ؓ mentions in his narration that he used to invoke blessings upon the Prophet ﷺ, as well as upon Abū Bakr and ʿUmar ؓ, as related by Mālik in *Al-Muwaṭṭaʾ* from the transmission of Yaḥyā al-Andalusī.[161] The sound meaning of this transmission is that he used to supplicate for Abū Bakr and ʿUmar ؓ.[162]

---

158 Related by Ṭabarānī in *Al-Ṣaghīr* and *Al-Awsaṭ*, Ibn Lāl, Tammām, ʿUqaylī, Ḥākim in his *Tārīkh*, Bayhaqī, and Ibn Mardawayh. Haythamī said in *Majmaʿ al-Zawāʾid* (10/269): "Its chain contains Nūḥ ibn Abī Maryam, who is a weak narrator." Munāwī said in *Fayḍ al-Qadīr* (1/56): "Bayhaqī said: 'It is a hadith that is not permitted to be used as a proof.' Ibn Ḥajar said: 'Related by Ṭabarānī from Anas, and its chain is very flimsy, and reported by Bayhaqī from Jābir with a weak narration and chain.' Sakhāwī said: 'All its chains are weak.'" Graded weak by Suyūṭī in *Al-Jāmiʿ al-Ṣaghīr* (15). Al-Ḥūt al-Bayrūtī said in *Asnā al-Maṭālib*, p. 11: "Related by Tammām and Daylamī with weak chains." Sakhāwī said in *Al-Maqāṣid al-Ḥasanah* (3): "However, it has many supporting evidences."
159 Reported by Bukhārī (5048) and Muslim (793/236) from Abū Mūsā al-Ashʿarī.
160 Reported by Mālik in *Al-Muwaṭṭaʾ* (1/165) from the chain of Mālik reported by Bukhārī (3369) and Muslim (407).
161 Reported by Mālik in *Al-Muwaṭṭaʾ* (1/166) and its chain is ṣaḥīḥ.
162 Reported by Bayhaqī in *Al-Sunan al-Kubrā* (5/245) from Ibn Bukayr, from Mālik, [who related] that ʿAbdullāh ibn Dīnār said, "I saw Ibn ʿUmar…", and he

Ibn Wahb related from Anas ibn Mālik: "We used to supplicate for our companions in their absence. We would say: 'O Allah! Place from You upon So-and-so the blessings of righteous people, the ones who stand in prayer by night and fast by day.'"

The view that the verifiers adopted and that I incline towards is what was stated by Mālik and Sufyān, related from Ibn ʿAbbās ﷺ, and favoured by several jurisprudents and rationalists, that one should not send blessings on people other than Prophets when they are mentioned, and that rather this is something specially designated for when Prophets are mentioned as a way of respecting and honouring them. Exalting, sanctifying, and magnifying are things we only do in regard to Allah Exalted and no-one else, and likewise, it is mandated that we specify the Prophet ﷺ and other Prophets for invoking blessings and sending salutations and not do that for anyone else. As Allah Exalted commanded in His statement: "Invoke the Blessings of Allah upon him, and salute him with worthy greetings of peace."[163]

For other imams and scholars, we mention the Forgiveness and Pleasure [of Allah]. As Allah Exalted said: "[They] pray, 'Our Lord! Forgive us and our fellow believers who preceded us in faith.'"[164]

And: "As for the foremost – the first of the Muhājirūn and the Anṣār – and those who follow them in goodness, Allah is pleased with them."[165]

Furthermore, this matter (i.e., invoking blessings on other than Prophets) was not known in the early period, as Abū ʿImrān[166] stated, but rather was introduced by Shias for some of their imams. They invoke blessings upon these imams when they are mentioned, and in doing so put them on the same level as the Prophet ﷺ. Resembling the people of innovation is forbidden, and it is essential to differ from them in their adherence to this practice.

The mention of invoking blessings upon the family and wives of the Prophet ﷺ is because of their connection to him, not as a way of singling them out.

---

mentions the narration. Declared sound by the present author.

163 *al-Aḥzāb*, 56.

164 *al-Ḥashr*, 10.

165 *al-Tawbah*, 100.

166 Abū ʿImrān al-Fāsī.

The scholars stated that when the Prophet ﷺ invoked blessings upon someone, it entailed supplicating or greeting rather than magnifying or honouring.

As the scholars pointed out, Allah Exalted says: "Do not call the Messenger [by his name] as you call one another."[167] Likewise, it is necessary for supplications for the Prophet ﷺ to differ from people's supplications for one another.

This was also the favoured opinion of Imam Abū al-Muẓaffar al-Isfarāyīnī,[168] one of our teachers, and Ibn ʿAbd al-Barr[169] followed the same view.

THE RULING ON VISITING THE GRAVE OF THE PROPHET ﷺ, THE VIRTUE OF THE PERSON WHO VISITS AND GREETS HIM, AND HOW A PERSON SHOULD GREET HIM AND SUPPLICATE FOR HIM

Visiting the grave of the Prophet ﷺ is one of the Sunnahs the Muslims are united upon, a grace that is eagerly sought after, and is related from Ibn ʿUmar ﷺ.

Qāḍī Abū ʿAlī narrated to us from Abū al-Faḍl ibn Khayrūn, from al-Ḥasan ibn Jaʿfar, from Abū al-Ḥasan ʿAlī ibn ʿUmar al-Dāraquṭnī, from Qāḍī al-Maḥāmilī, from Muhammad ibn ʿAbd al-Razzāq, from Mūsā ibn Hilāl, from ʿAbdullāh ibn ʿUmar, from Nāfiʿ, from Ibn ʿUmar, who said: "The Prophet ﷺ said: 'My intercession is mandated for whoever visits my grave.'"[170]

---

167 *al-Nūr*, 63.

168 The eminent mufti, Ṭāhir ibn Muhammad al-Ṭūsī al-Shāfiʿī. He passed away in Ṭūs in 471 AH. His biography can be found in *Siyar Aʿlām al-Nubalā'* (18/401-402).

169 Yūsuf ibn ʿAbdillāh al-Qurṭubī al-Mālikī, author of *Al-Istīʿāb*, *Al-Istidhkār*, and *Al-Tamhīd*. He was born in 368 AH and passed away in 463 AH. His biography can be found in *Siyar Aʿlām al-Nubalā'* (18/153-163).

170 Reported here from Dāraquṭnī (2/278), but his chain includes "ʿUbaydullāh ibn Muhammad al-Warrāq" instead of "Muhammad ibn ʿAbd al-Razzāq". Also reported by Bazzār (1198), Ibn ʿAdiyy, Bayhaqī in *Shuʿab al-Īmān*, Ibn Khuzaymah in his *Ṣaḥīḥ* (without commenting on its authenticity), Ibn Abī al-Dunyā, Ṭabarānī, and Abū al-Shaykh. Mentioned by Haythamī in *Majmaʿ al-Zawā'id* (4/2), where he said: "It was related by Bazzār and the chain contains ʿAbdullāh ibn Ibrāhīm al-Ghifārī, who is a weak narrator." Graded weak by Suyūṭī in *Al-Jāmiʿ al-Ṣaghīr* (8715). Munāwī said in *Fayḍ al-Qadīr* (6/140): "Ibn

Anas ibn Mālik ؓ narrated: "The Messenger of Allah ﷺ said: 'Whoever visits me in Madinah hoping for reward will be close to me, and I will be an intercessor for them on the Day of Judgement.'"[171]

And in another narration: "Whoever visits me after my death is as if they had visited me during my life."[172]

Mālik disliked saying: "We visited the grave of the Prophet ﷺ." There was a difference of opinion regarding the meaning of this. Some said it is the word ["visited"] that is disliked, because of the

---

al-Qaṭṭān said: 'Its chain contains ʿAbdullāh ibn ʿUmar al-ʿUmarī.' Abū Ḥātim said: '[He is] unknown (majhūl).' The chain also contains Mūsā ibn Hilāl al-Baṣrī. ʿUqaylī said: 'His narrations are unsound and should not be followed.' Ibn al-Qaṭṭān said: 'The chain contains two weak narrators.' Nawawī said in *Al-Majmūʿ*: 'Very weak.' Firyābī said: 'Its chain contains Mūsā ibn Hilāl al-ʿAbdī.' ʿUqaylī said: 'His narrations should not be followed.' Abū Ḥātim said: '[He is] unknown.' Subkī said: '[He is] ḥasan or ṣaḥīḥ.' Dhahabī said: 'All its chains are weak, but they strengthen each other.' Ibn Ḥajar said: 'A gharīb narration.' In summary, Ibn Taymiyyah said in *Al-Fatāwā* (27/29): '[It is] fabricated and incorrect.'" Suyūṭī said in *Al-Manāhil*, p. 1115: "It has chains and supporting evidence that prompted Dhahabī to grade the narration ḥasan." Subkī has a book entitled *Shifāʾ al-Siqām fī Ziyārah Khayr al-Anām*, in which he responds to the calls of Shaykh al-Islām Ibn Taymiyyah regarding the narrations about visiting the Prophet ﷺ, and he was supported by Ibn ʿAbd al-Hādī in his book *Al-Ṣārim al-Munkī*. See also *Al-Maqāṣid al-Ḥasanah* (1125) by Sakhāwī.

171 Attributed by Suyūṭī in *Al-Jāmiʿ al-Ṣaghīr* (8716) to Bayhaqī in *Shuʿab al-Īmān*, and he graded the narration ḥasan. Munāwī disagreed in *Fayḍ al-Qadīr* (6/141), where he said: "The author's grading of ḥasan is incorrect, for it contains weak narrators." Mentioned, with "*shifāʾ*" being used in the context of nursing and caring for rather than interceding, by Mundhirī in *Al-Targhīb wa al-Tarhīb* (2/224).

172 Reported here from Dāraquṭnī (2/278) from Hārūn Abū Qazaʿah, from a man from the family of Ḥāṭib, from Ḥāṭib. Attributed by Mundhirī in *Al-Targhīb wa al-Tarhīb* (2/224) to Bayhaqī. Attributed by Suyūṭī in *Al-Manāhil*, p. 1117, to Saʿīd ibn Manṣūr in his *Sunan*, Dāraquṭnī (2/278), Bayhaqī in *Al-Sunan al-Kubrā* (5/246), and Ṭabarānī, from Ibn ʿUmar. Haythamī said in *Majmaʿ al-Zawāʾid* (4/2): "It was related by Ṭabarānī in *Al-Kabīr* and *Al-Awsaṭ* and the chain contains Ḥafṣ ibn Abī Dāwūd al-Qārī. Aḥmad said he is reliable, and a group of scholars said he is weak." Dhahabī said, as found in *Al-Maqāṣid al-Ḥasanah*, p. 413: "And the narration with one of the best chains was the narration of Ḥāṭib."

statement the Prophet ﷺ that is related: "Allah Exalted curses the visitors of graves."[173]

[However,] this is refuted by the saying of the Prophet ﷺ: "I forbade you from visiting graves, but now you can visit them."[174] Also, the Prophet ﷺ said, "Whoever visits my grave",[175] using the word "visit".

Others said that Mālik disliked saying it because they used to say that the visitor is better than the visited. This also has no basis, for not every visitor is of this type and it is not a general rule. It is related in the hadith about the people of Paradise that they will visit their Lord, and the word "visit" was not prevented from being used in relation to the rights of Allah Exalted.[176]

Abū ʿImrān said: "Rather, Mālik disliked for 'the circumambulation of the visit' or 'we visited the grave of the Prophet ﷺ' because these were the phrases the people used for visiting each other, and he disliked putting the Prophet ﷺ on the same level as the people by using the same wording. Instead, he preferred for the Prophet ﷺ to be singled out by saying: 'We conveyed greetings upon the Prophet ﷺ.'"

Furthermore, for people to visit each other is merely permissible, whereas travelling to the grave of the Prophet ﷺ is strongly mandated. "Mandated" here refers to something that is recommended, desired, and emphasized, rather than the jurisprudential ruling.

For me, the most accurate interpretation is that what Mālik discouraged and disliked was the inclusion of "the grave of the Prophet ﷺ" in the wording, and that if someone said, "We visited the Prophet ﷺ", he would not have disliked that. This is because of the statement of the Prophet ﷺ, "O Allah! Do not allow my grave to become an idol that is

---

173 Reported with this wording by Abū Yaʿlā (5908) from Abū Hurayrah. Also reported by Aḥmad (2/337), Tirmidhī (1056), Ibn Mājah (1576), and others with the wording: "The Messenger of Allah ﷺ cursed women who visit graves." Tirmidhī said: "This hadith is *ḥasan ṣaḥīḥ*." Authenticated by Ibn Ḥibbān in *Mawārid al-Ẓamʾān* (789), where its referencing can be found. Suyūṭī said the word "*zuwwārāt*" refers to visitors, whereas Mullā al-Qārī (3/512) said that it should be "*zawwārāt*" and refers to those who visit excessively.

174 Reported by Muslim (977) from Buraydah.

175 Reported by Dāraquṭnī (2/278).

176 The narration about visiting [the Prophet ﷺ] was reported by Tirmidhī (2549) and Ibn Mājah (4336) from Abū Hurayrah. Tirmidhī said: "This hadith is *ḥasan gharīb*."

worshipped after me. The Anger of Allah was severe upon people who took the graves of their Prophets as places of prostration (*masājid*)."[177] Mālik effaced the connection of [even] the word "grave" to the phrase, removing any resemblance to such people and cutting off the means and shutting the door to such an action, and Allah knows best.

Isḥāq ibn Ibrāhīm al-Faqīh said: "One of the [ancient] practices of Hajj that remains is to travel to Madinah, aiming to pray in the Mosque of the Messenger of Allah ﷺ, seeking the blessings of seeing his Purified Garden[178], his pulpit, his grave; the places he sat, touched, and rested his feet; and the post he used to lean against, where Jibrīl would descend upon him with Revelation; as well as [seeking the blessings of] the Companions and imams of the Muslims who used to visit. All these things should be given consideration."

Ibn Abī Fudayk[179] said: "I heard one of the people I came across saying: 'It has reached us that whoever stands by should recite the following verse: "Indeed, Allah showers His Blessings upon the Prophet, and His Angels pray for him."[180] Then, they should say: "May Allah send His Blessings upon you, O Muhammad!" Whoever says that seventy times will be called by an Angel, "May Allah send His Blessings upon you, O So-and-so", and every need of theirs will be dealt with.'"

Yazīd ibn Abī Saʿīd al-Mahrī said: "I went to ʿUmar ibn ʿAbd al-ʿAzīz. When I bade him farewell, he said to me: 'There is something you need to do.'

'What is it?' I asked.

'When you get to Madinah, you will see the grave of the Prophet ﷺ. Convey my greetings to him', he replied."[181]

---

177 Reported by Mālik in *Al-Muwaṭṭā'* (1/172) from ʿAṭā' ibn Yasār in a *mursal* narration. Also found in a sound, *mawṣūl* narration from Abū Hurayrah.

178 Translator's note: The Rawḍah.

179 The trustworthy imam, Muhammad ibn Ismāʿīl ibn Muslim ibn Abī Fudayk. Sakhāwī said: "He passed away in 200 AH." His biography can be found in *Siyar Aʿlām al-Nubalā'* (9/486-487).

180 *al-Aḥzāb*, 56.

181 Mentioned by Sakhāwī in *Al-Qawl al-Badīʿ*, p. 304, where he said: "Reported by Ibn Abī al-Dunyā, and from the same chain by Bayhaqī in *Shuʿab al-Īmān*."

Others said that ʿUmar ibn ʿAbd al-ʿAzīz would send an envoy from al-Shām to convey his greetings to the Prophet ﷺ.[182]

One [narrator] said: "I saw Anas ibn Mālik come to the grave of the Prophet ﷺ, stop, and raise his hands, and I thought he was about to start praying. [Instead,] he greeted the Prophet ﷺ and then left."

Mālik said, in the transmission of Ibn Wahb, that when a person greets the Prophet ﷺ and supplicates, they should stand and face his noble grave rather than the Qiblah, and then approach and supplicate but not touch the grave with their hand.

He also said, in *Al-Mabsūṭ*: "I do not think people should stand by the grave of the Prophet ﷺ and supplicate. Rather, they should greet him and then continue on their way."

Ibn Abī Mulaykah[183] said: "Whoever wishes to stand facing the Prophet ﷺ should make it so that the lamp in the direction of the Qiblah is by his head."

Nāfiʿ[184] said: "Ibn ʿUmar used to convey his greetings at the grave. I saw him come to the grave one hundred times or more and say: 'May peace be upon you, O Prophet. May peace be upon you, O Abū Bakr. May peace be upon my father.' Then, he would leave."

Ibn ʿUmar would place his hand on the spot the Prophet ﷺ would sit upon on the pulpit. Then, he would place his hand on his face.[185]

It was related from Ibn Qusayṭ[186] and al-ʿUtbī[187] that when the mosque was empty, the Companions of the Prophet ﷺ would hold

---

182 Reported by Bayhaqī in *Shuʿab al-Īmān* from Ḥātim ibn Wardān.

183 The reliable Follower and expert in jurisprudence, ʿAbdullāh ibn ʿUbaydillāh ibn Abī Mulaykah. He died in 117 AH. Dhahabī said: "He was in his eighties." His biography can be found in *Siyar Aʿlām al-Nubalā'* (5/88-90).

184 The trustworthy Follower and well-known jurist, Abū ʿAbdillāh al-Madanī, the servant of Ibn ʿUmar. He passed away either in 117 AH or after that. His biography can be found in *Siyar Aʿlām al-Nubalā'* (5/95-101).

185 Reported by Tirmidhī (3380), Aḥmad (2/446), and others.

186 The imam, jurist, Follower, and reliable narrator, Yazīd ibn ʿAbdillāh ibn Qusayṭ al-Madanī. He passed away in 122 AH at the age of ninety. His biography can be found in *Siyar Aʿlām al-Nubalā'* (5/266).

187 The jurist of Andalusia, Muhammad ibn Aḥmad al-Umawī al-Sufyānī. A Mālikī [in jurisprudence], he was the author of *Al-ʿUtbiyyah*. He passed away in either 254 or 255 AH. His biography can be found in *Siyar Aʿlām al-Nubalā'* (12/335-336).

onto the knob[188] of the pulpit which was by the grave with their right hand. Then, they would face the Qiblah and supplicate.[189]

The transmission of Yaḥyā ibn Yaḥyā al-Laythī related in *Al-Muwaṭṭā'* mentions that he would stand at the grave of the Prophet ﷺ and invoke blessings upon him, upon Abū Bakr, and upon ʿUmar.[190]

[Or,] according to Ibn al-Qāsim and al-Qaʿnabī[191]: "...and supplicate for Abū Bakr and ʿUmar."[192]

Mālik said, in the transmission of Ibn Wahb: "The greeter should say: 'May peace be upon you, O Prophet, and the Mercy and Blessings of Allah.'" And he said in *Al-Mabsūṭ*: "...and they should greet Abū Bakr and ʿUmar."

Qāḍī Abū al-Walīd al-Bājī[193] said: "In my opinion, they should supplicate for the Prophet ﷺ with the wording of the invocation of blessings, and for Abū Bakr and ʿUmar with an alternative [wording],[194] as detailed in the narration of Ibn ʿUmar."

Ibn Ḥabīb said: "When a person enters the mosque of the Messenger ﷺ, they should say: 'In the Name of Allah, may peace be upon the Messenger of Allah, may peace be upon us from our Lord, may Allah send His Blessings upon Muhammad, and may His Angels pray for him. O Allah, forgive me for my sins, open the gates of Your Mercy and Paradise to me, and protect me from the accursed Shayṭān.' Then, they should proceed to the Purified Garden – which is the area between the grave and the pulpit – and perform two units of prayer before standing at the grave, praising Allah in both [units] and asking Him to help you complete what you set out to do. It is acceptable to

---

188 Translator's note: It is called a "*rummānah*" because it is shaped like a pomegranate.

189 The hadith of Ibn Qusayṭ was related by Ibn Saʿd. See *Al-Manāhil*, p. 1123.

190 Reported by Mālik in *Al-Muwaṭṭa'* (1/166).

191 ʿAbdullāh ibn Maslamah in Qaʿnab, a devoted and exemplary imam and one of the narrators of *Al-Muwaṭṭa'* from Imam Mālik. He was born in 130 AH in Yasīr, and passed away in 221 AH. His biography can be found in *Siyar Aʿlām al-Nubalā'* (10/257-264).

192 Reported by Bayhaqī in *Al-Sunan al-Kubrā* (5/245).

193 The imam, scholar, *ḥāfiẓ*, and polymath, Sulaymān ibn Khalaf al-Andalusī. He was born in 403 AH and passed away in 473 AH. His biography can be found in *Siyar Aʿlām al-Nubalā'* (18/535-545).

194 Translator's note: i.e., with an invocation of peace.

perform the two units outside of the Purified Garden, but inside the Purified Garden is preferred.

The Prophet ﷺ said: 'The area between my room and pulpit is a Purified Garden from the Gardens of Paradise, and my pulpit is upon a stream from the streams of Paradise.'[195]

Then, you should stand at the grave with humility and respect, send blessings upon him, praise him with whatever comes to you, and [then] greet Abū Bakr and ʿUmar and supplicate for them.

Increase in invoking blessings in the Mosque of the Prophet ﷺ during the night and during the day, and do not neglect visiting Qubā' Mosque[196] and the graves of the martyrs."

Mālik said in his letter to Muhammad[197]: "And greet the Prophet ﷺ when you enter and leave (i.e., in Madinah) and in the time between."

Muhammad said: "When you leave, spend the last part of your time there standing at the grave. Likewise for the person who is embarking on a journey."

Ibn Wahb related from Fāṭimah, the daughter of the Prophet ﷺ, that the Prophet ﷺ said: "If you enter the mosque, send blessings upon the Prophet ﷺ and say: 'O Allah! Forgive me for my sins and open the gates of Your Mercy to me.' And when you leave, send blessings upon the Prophet ﷺ and say: 'O Allah! Forgive me for my sins and open the gates of Your Grace to me.'"[198]

---

195 Reported by Abū Yaʿlā (118) and Bazzār (1194) from Abū Bakr al-Ṣiddīq. Haythamī said in *Majmaʿ al-Zawā'id* (4/9): "Its chain contains Abū Bakr ibn Abī Sabrah, who is a prolific fabricator." The first part of the narration is reported by Bukhārī (1195) and Muslim (1390) from ʿAbdullāh ibn Zayd al-Māzinī, and by Bukhārī (1196) and Muslim (1391) from Abū Hurayrah. The last part of the narration is reported by Aḥmad (5/335) and Ṭabarānī from Sahl ibn Saʿd. Haythamī said in *Majmaʿ al-Zawā'id* (4/9): "Aḥmad's narrators are *ṣaḥīḥ*." See *Majmaʿ al-Zawā'id* (4/8-9).

196 Qubā' was a village in the province of Madinah where the mosque founded on righteousness was established. Today, it is a neighbourhood of al-Madinah al-Munawwarah.

197 Muhammad ibn al-Mawwāz, one of the great Mālikī jurisprudents. He passed away in 269 AH. His biography can be found in *Siyar Aʿlām al-Nubalā'* (13/6).

This could also be referring to Mālikī jurist Muhammad ibn Maslamah, who passed away in 216 AH. His biography can be found in *Nasīm al-Riyāḍ* (3/468).

198 Reported by Bukhārī (3544) and Muslim (2343).

Another transmission says "greet" instead of "send blessings upon", and states that one should say when leaving: "O Allah! I ask You for Your Grace."[199]

And in another narration: "O Allah! Protect me from the accursed Shayṭān."[200]

Muhammad ibn Sīrīn related: "When the people entered the mosque, they would say: 'May Allah send His Blessings upon Muhammad, and may His Angels pray for him. May peace be upon you, O Prophet, and the Mercy and Blessings of Allah. In the Name of Allah we have entered, in the Name of Allah we will leave, and upon Allah we rely.'

It was also related from Fāṭimah that when the Prophet ﷺ entered the mosque, he would say: 'May Allah send His Blessings upon Muhammad, and worthy greetings of peace.'"[201] Then, he mentioned the same as is found in the narration of Fāṭimah related above.

In another transmission, [we find]: "He praised Allah, pronounced His Name, and invoked blessings upon the Prophet ﷺ", and the same is mentioned.[202]

And in another transmission, [the Prophet ﷺ said]: "In the Name of Allah, and may peace be upon the Messenger of Allah."[203]

---

199 Reported by Abū Dāwūd (465) and others from Abū Ḥumayd or Abū Usayd al-Anṣārī. Nawawī authenticated its chain in *Al-Adhkār* (92) with my commentary, and the last part of the narration is reported by Muslim (713).

200 Reported by Nasā'ī in *ʿAmal al-Yawm wa al-Laylah* (92) from Abū Hurayrah, from Kaʿb al-Aḥbār and Muslim (2343). Also reported, with its transmissions, by Ibn Mājah (773), Nasā'ī in *ʿAmal al-Yawm wa al-Laylah* (90), and Ibn al-Sunnī (86), in a *marfūʿ* narration from Abū Hurayrah. Authenticated by Ibn Ḥibbān in *Mawārid al-Ẓam'ān* (321), Ibn Khuzaymah (452), and Būṣīrī in *Miṣbāḥ al-Zujājah* (1/97). Also authenticated by Ḥākim (1/207), and Dhahabī concurred. The transmissions of Ibn Mājah and Ibn al-Sunnī say "Safeguard me"; those mentioned by Ibn Khuzaymah, Ibn Ḥibbān, and Ḥākim say "Shelter me", and the narration related by Nasā'ī says "Distance me". Another transmission related by Ibn al-Sunnī says: "Grant me refuge".

201 Reported by Tirmidhī (314) and Aḥmad (6/282, 283), with the wording: "When he entered the mosque, he would invoke blessings and send salutations upon Muhammad."

202 Reported by Ibn al-Sunnī (87).

203 Reported by Ibn Mājah (771) and Aḥmad (6/283).

Others narrated that when the Prophet ﷺ entered the mosque, he would say: "O Allah! Open the gates of Your Mercy to me, and ease for me the gates to Your provision."[204]

Abū Hurayrah ؓ narrated: "The Messenger of Allah ﷺ said: 'If one of you enters the mosque, they should send blessings upon the Prophet ﷺ, and then say: "O Allah! Open the gates of Your Mercy to me..."'"[205]

Mālik said in *Al-Mabsūṭ*: "It is not necessary for the people of Madinah who enter and leave the mosque to stand at the grave of the Prophet ﷺ. Rather, that is for visitors."

He also said: "There is no problem with a person who has returned from a journey or is embarking on a journey standing at the grave of the Prophet ﷺ, sending blessings upon him, and supplicating for him and for Abū Bakr and ʿUmar."

He was told: "There are some from the people of Madinah who are neither embarking on nor returning from a journey, yet they do that once or more within a day, standing on Fridays or other days once, twice, or more by the grave, greeting and supplicating for an hour."

He replied: "This has not reached me from any of the scholars of jurisprudence in our land, and it is permissible to leave it. The later generations of this community will only be rectified by what rectified the earlier generations, and it has not reached me that the earliest generations used to do that. It is disliked except for a person who has arrived from, or is embarking on, a journey."

Ibn al-Qāsim said: "I saw that whenever the people of Madinah left or entered, they would go to the grave and convey greetings, but that is [merely based on] opinion."

Al-Bājī said: "A distinction was made between the people of Madinah and visitors, for visitors come with the intention of doing that, whereas the people of Madinah live there rather than coming to the city with the intention of [visiting] the grave and [conveying] greetings."

The Prophet ﷺ said: "O Allah! Do not allow my grave to become an idol that is worshipped after me. The Anger of Allah was severe upon

---

204 Related by Suyūṭī in *Al-Manāhil*, p. 1129, without mentioning its reference.

205 Reported by Ibn Mājah (773), Nasāʾī in *ʿAmal al-Yawm wa al-Laylah* (90), and Ibn al-Sunnī (86).

people who took the graves of their Prophets as places of prostration (*masājid*)."[206]

And: "Do not make my grave a gathering place (*ʿīd*)."[207]

In the writing of Aḥmad ibn Saʿīd al-Hindī about those who stand at the grave, he said: "Do not hang onto it, touch it, or stand by it for a long time."

And in *Al-ʿUtbiyyah*[208], [we find]: "One should start with prayer before the greeting in the Mosque of the Messenger of Allah ﷺ. The best place there for supererogatory prayer is the prayer place of the Prophet ﷺ, where the post scented with *khalūq*[209] is located. As for the obligatory prayers, they should move forward to the rows. And to me, performing supererogatory prayers there is better for travellers than in their homes."

THE ETIQUETTES REQUIRED OF THE PERSON WHO ENTERS THE MOSQUE OF THE PROPHET ﷺ, BESIDES WHAT WE HAVE ALREADY MENTIONED, THE VIRTUE OF THE MOSQUE AND PRAYING IN IT, THE VIRTUE OF PRAYING IN THE MOSQUE OF MAKKAH, A MENTION OF THE GRAVE AND PULPIT OF THE PROPHET ﷺ, AND THE VIRTUE OF RESIDING IN MADINAH AND MAKKAH

Allah Exalted said: "Certainly, a mosque founded on righteousness from the first day is more worthy of your prayers."[210]

It is related that the Prophet ﷺ was asked: "Which mosque is it?" He replied: "It is this mosque of mine."[211]

---

206 Reported by Mālik in *Al-Muwaṭṭā'* (1/172) from ʿAṭā' ibn Yasār in a *mursal* narration. Also found in a sound, *mawṣūl* narration from Abū Hurayrah.

207 Reported by Abū Dāwūd (2042), Aḥmad (2/367), and others, from Abū Hurayrah. Nawawī authenticated its chain in *Riyāḍ al-Ṣāliḥīn* (1461) with my commentary. Ibn Ḥajar said in *Takhrīj al-Adhkār*: "A *ḥasan* narration." Attributed in *Jāmiʿ al-Uṣūl* (4/406) to Nasā'ī. Also reported by Abū Yaʿlā (469) from ʿAlī.

208 A book on Mālikī jurisprudence by Muhammad ibn Aḥmad al-Sufyānī.

209 A fragrance made from saffron and other ingredients.

210 *al-Tawbah*, 108.

211 Reported by Muslim (1398).

This was the opinion followed by Ibn al-Musayyib, Zayd ibn Thābit, Ibn ʿUmar, Mālik ibn Anas, and others. Ibn ʿAbbās narrated that it refers to the Qubā' Mosque.[212]

I read the following hadith to Hishām ibn Aḥmad al-Faqīh, who narrated from al-Ḥusayn ibn Muhammad al-Ḥāfiẓ, from Abū ʿUmar al-Namarī, from Abū Muhammad ibn ʿAbd al-Mu'min, from Abū Bakr ibn Dāsah, from Abū Dāwūd, from Musaddad, from Sufyān, from al-Zuhrī, from Saʿīd ibn al-Musayyib, from Abū Hurayrah, who said: "The Prophet ﷺ said: 'A [specific] journey should not be made[213] to any mosque except three: the Sacred Mosque, this mosque of mine, and al-Aqsa Mosque.'"[214]

We have already mentioned invoking blessings and peace upon the Prophet ﷺ when entering the mosque.

ʿAbdullāh ibn ʿAmr ibn al-ʿĀṣ narrated that when the Prophet ﷺ entered the mosque, he would say: "I seek refuge in Allah, the Greatest, His Noble Face, and His Eternal Authority, from the accursed Shayṭān."[215]

Mālik said: "ʿUmar ibn al-Khaṭṭāb heard a voice in the mosque, so he called over the person. 'Which tribe are you from?' he asked.

'I am a man from the Thaqīf', he replied.

ʿUmar said: 'If you were from these two towns (i.e., Makkah or Madinah), I would have disciplined you. Voices should not be raised in this mosque of ours.'"[216]

Muhammad ibn Maslamah said: "It is not appropriate for anyone to raise their voice in the mosque or do anything to harm it, and they should keep themselves away from what is disliked."

---

212 Related by Ibn Abī Ḥātim. See *Al-Manāhil*, p. 1133.

213 Translator's note: lit., "the saddlebags should not be fastened".

214 Reported here from Abū Dāwūd (2033). Also reported by Bukhārī (1189) and Muslim (1397).

215 Reported by Abū Dāwūd (466). Nawawī said in *Al-Adhkār* (94) with my commentary: "A *ḥasan* narration. Related by Abū Dāwūd with a good (*jayyid*) chain." Also graded *ḥasan* by Ibn Ḥajar in *Takhrīj al-Adhkār*.

216 Reported by Bukhārī (470) from al-Sā'ib ibn Yazīd from ʿUmar.

This was all reported by Qāḍī Ismāʿīl[217] in *Al-Mabsūṭ* in the chapter on the virtue of the Mosque of the Prophet ﷺ, and all scholars agree that other mosques are subject to the same rulings.

Qāḍī Ismāʿīl mentioned: "Muhammad ibn Maslamah[218] said: 'In the Mosque of the Messenger ﷺ, it is disliked to raise one's voice in a way that will distract the congregation from their prayers. It was also disliked to raise one's voice in reciting the *talbiyah* except in the Sacred Mosque and Minā Mosque.'"

Abū Hurayrah ؓ narrated that the Prophet ﷺ said: "A prayer in this mosque of mine is better than one thousand prayers in any other, except the Sacred Mosque."[219]

The people differed as to whether this signifies that Makkah or Madinah is more virtuous. In the transmission related from him by Ashhab, Mālik took the opinion, and a group of his companions including Ibn Nāfiʿ[220] said the same, that the meaning of the narration is that a prayer in the Mosque of the Prophet ﷺ is still better than a prayer in the Sacred Mosque, but less than one thousand times better. They used as evidence what was related from ʿUmar ibn al-Khaṭṭāb ؓ, that a prayer in the Sacred Mosque is better than one hundred prayers in any other.[221] Therefore, they concluded, a prayer in the Mosque of the Prophet ﷺ is nine hundred times better than a prayer in the Sacred Mosque, and one thousand times better than a prayer in any other. This view of Madinah's merit over Makkah was also followed by ʿUmar ibn al-Khaṭṭāb ؓ, Mālik, and most of the people of Madinah.

The people of Kufa and Makkah considered Makkah superior. From the companions of Mālik, this was the view of ʿAṭāʾ, Ibn Wahb, and Ibn

---

217 The imam, esteemed scholar, and *ḥāfiẓ*, Shaykh al-Islām Abū Isḥāq Ismāʿīl ibn Isḥāq al-Baṣrī al-Mālikī. He was born in 199 AH and passed away in 282 AH. His works include *Faḍl al-Ṣalāh ʿalā al-Nabī* ﷺ and *Al-Mabsūṭ* in jurisprudence. His biography can be found in *Siyar Aʿlām al-Nubalāʾ* (13/339-341).

218 A Mālikī jurist.

219 Reported by Bukhārī (1190) and Muslim (1394).

220 ʿAbdullāh ibn Nāfiʿ al-Ṣāʾigh, one of the great jurisprudents of Madinah. He stuck to Imam Mālik vehemently. He was born in the early 120s AH and died in 206 AH. His biography can be found in *Siyar Aʿlām al-Nubalāʾ* (10/371-374).

221 Reported by Ḥumaydī in his *Musnad* (970). His commentator and our noble teacher Ḥusayn Asad said: "Its chain is *ṣaḥīḥ* and it is a *mawqūf* narration from ʿUmar."

Ḥabīb, and al-Sājī[222] related it from Shāfiʿī. They took the previously mentioned narration at face value and concluded that a prayer in the Sacred Mosque is of greater value. They used as their evidence the narration of ʿAbdullāh ibn al-Zubayr that the Prophet ﷺ said: "A prayer in the Sacred Mosque is better than one hundred prayers in this mosque of mine."[223] Qatādah narrated the same. According to this view, prayer in the Sacred Mosque is superior to prayer in any other.

There is no difference of opinion regarding the fact that the grave of the Prophet ﷺ is the best patch of earth in the world.

Qāḍī Abū al-Walīd al-Bājī said: "The narration signifies the difference between the ruling of Makkah and other mosques [in general]. It does not indicate the status of Makkah in relation to Madinah."

Al-Ṭaḥāwī took the view that this superiority was regarding obligatory prayers, whereas Muṭarrif believed that it applied to supererogatory prayers as well. ʿAbd al-Razzāq mentioned a similar narration regarding the superiority of Ramadan in Madinah.[224]

The Prophet ﷺ said: "The area between my room and pulpit is a Purified Garden from the Gardens of Paradise."[225]

---

222 Zakariyyā ibn Yaḥyā al-Sājī al-Shāfiʿī, the devoted imam and *ḥāfiẓ*. He died in Basra in 307 AH in his nineties. His biography can be found in *Siyar Aʿlām al-Nubalā'* (14/197-200).

223 Reported by Aḥmad (4/5) and others. Authenticated by Ibn Ḥibbān in *Mawārid al-Ẓam'ān* (1027), where its referencing can be found. The narration of Abū Hurayrah was reported by Bukhārī (1190) and Muslim (1394).

224 Also reported by Ṭabarānī in *Al-Kabīr* in a narration from Bilāl ibn al-Ḥārith that he deemed *marfūʿ*: "A Ramadan in Madinah is better than one thousand Ramadans in any other city, and a Friday in Madinah is better than one thousand Fridays in any other city." Haythamī said in *Majmaʿ al-Zawā'id* (3/145): "Its chain contains Kathīr ibn ʿAbdillāh, who is a weak narrator." Graded sound by Suyūṭī in *Al-Jāmiʿ al-Ṣaghīr* (4480), where he extends its attribution to al-Ḍiyā' in *Al-Mukhtārah*. Mentioned by Dhahabī in *Al-Mīzān*, where he said: "This is false, and its chain is obscure…and al-Ḍiyā' did not bring its referencing in *Al-Mukhtārah*."

225 Reported by Bukhārī (1195) and Muslim (1390) from ʿAbdullāh ibn Zayd al-Māzinī.

The same was narrated by Abū Hurayrah and Abū Saʿīd, with the Prophet ﷺ adding: "…and my pulpit is upon my Fount."[226]

And in another hadith: "and my pulpit is upon a stream from the streams of Paradise."[227]

Ṭabarī said: "This has two possible meanings. Firstly, 'house' could be taken at face value and refer to his residence. This is clarified in another transmission related from the Prophet ﷺ, in which he said: '…between my room and my pulpit.'[228]

Secondly, this 'house' could be his grave." This was Zayd ibn Aslam's interpretation of this narration. As was related [from the Prophet ﷺ]: "…between my grave and my pulpit."[229]

Ṭabarī said: "As his grave is inside his house, the meanings of the two transmissions coincide and there is no contradiction between them. His grave is inside his room, which was also his house."

The statement of the Prophet ﷺ, "and my pulpit is upon my Fount", carries a few possible meanings. The first is that it refers to his pulpit in this world, and this is the most apparent meaning, the second is that he has a pulpit in the Hereafter, and the third is that by his "pulpit" and attendance at it he meant adherence to righteous deeds, which mandates that one will attend and drink from the Fount, and this was the view of al-Bājī.

His statement, "a Purified Garden from the Gardens of Paradise", carries two possible meanings. The first is that the area mandates that, and that supplicating and praying within the space is worthy of that as a reward. This is similar to the saying: "Paradise is beneath the shade of the sword."[230] The second possible meaning is that exact patch of the mosque has been transferred by Allah and will be in Paradise, and this was the view of al-Dāwūdī.

---

226 Reported by Mālik in *Al-Muwaṭṭa'* (1/197). Also reported by Bukhārī (1196) and Muslim (1391) from Abū Hurayrah.

227 A portion of the hadith reported by Abū Yaʿlā (118) and Bazzār (1194).

228 Reported by Aḥmad (3/389) and Abū Yaʿlā (1784) from Jābir ibn ʿAbdillāh. Haythamī said in *Majmaʿ al-Zawā'id* (4/8): "Its chain contains ʿAlī ibn Zayd. There is some discussion about him, and some have said that he is reliable."

229 Reported by Aḥmad (3/64) and Abū Yaʿlā (1341) from Abū Saʿīd al-Khudrī, and reported by Bazzār (430) from ʿAlī and Abū Hurayrah.

230 Reported by Bukhārī (2818) and Muslim (1742) in a *marfūʿ* narration from ʿAbdullāh ibn Abī Awfā.

Ibn ʿUmar and a group of the Companions narrated that the Prophet ﷺ said about Madinah: "Anyone who patiently endures its hardships and intense difficulties, I will be a witness – or intercessor – for them on the Day of Judgement."[231]

The Prophet ﷺ said about those who left Madinah: "And Madinah is better for them, if only they knew."[232]

He also said: "Madinah is like a furnace. It expels its impurities and clarifies what is pure."[233]

And: "No-one leaves Madinah out of disinclination for it except that Allah gives the city someone better than him."[234]

It was related that the Prophet ﷺ said: "[For] whoever dies in one of the two sacred sites whilst performing Hajj or ʿumrah, Allah will raise them on the Day of Judgement with no account and no punishment [due] upon them."[235]

And in another transmission: "...will be raised amongst those who are safe and secure on the Day of Judgement."[236]

Ibn ʿUmar narrated that the Prophet ﷺ said: "Whoever is able to die in Madinah should do so, for I will intercede for whoever dies in the city."[237]

---

231 Reported by Muslim (1377) from Ibn ʿUmar. See also *Jāmiʿ al-Uṣūl* (9/313-317).

232 Reported by Bukhārī (1875) and Muslim (1388) from Sufyān ibn Abī Zuhayr.

233 Reported by Bukhārī (1883) and Muslim (1383) from Jābir ibn ʿAbdillāh.

234 Reported by Mālik in *Al-Muwaṭṭa'* (2/887) and ʿAbd al-Razzāq in *Al-Muṣannaf* (17160) in a *mursal* narration from ʿUrwah. Reported in a similar form by Muslim (1363) from Saʿd ibn Abī Waqqāṣ, and (1381) from Abū Hurayrah.

235 Reported by Bayhaqī in *Al-Sunan al-Kubrā* and Dāraquṭnī (2/297-298) from ʿĀ'ishah with a weak chain. See *Al-Manāhil*, p. 1149. See also *Majmaʿ al-Zawā'id* (2/319).

236 Related by Ṭabarānī in *Al-Kabīr* from Salmān. Haythamī said in *Majmaʿ al-Zawā'id* (2/319): "Its chain contains ʿAbd al-Ghaffār ibn Saʿīd, who is not taken from (*matrūk*)." Also related by Ṭabarānī in *Al-Ṣaghīr* and *Al-Awsaṭ* from Jābir ibn ʿAbdillāh. Haythamī said in *Majmaʿ al-Zawā'id* (2/319): "Its chain contains Mūsā ibn ʿAbd al-Raḥmān al-Masrūqī, who was mentioned by Ibn Ḥibbān in *Al-Thiqāt* (meaning: "the reliable ones"), and ʿAbdullāh ibn al-Mu'ammal, who was declared reliable by Ibn Ḥibbān and others and weak by Aḥmad and others, and its chain is *ḥasan*." Also reported by Bayhaqī in *Al-Sunan al-Kubrā* from ʿUmar. See *Al-Manāhil*, p. 1149.

237 Reported by Tirmidhī (3917) and Ibn Mājah (3112) in a *marfūʿ* narration from Ibn ʿUmar. Tirmidhī said: "This hadith is *ḥasan gharīb*." Authenticated by Ibn

And Allah Exalted said: "Surely the first House [of worship] established for humanity is the one at Bakkah – a blessed sanctuary and a guide for [all] people. In it are clear signs and the standing-place of Ibrāhīm. Whoever enters it should be safe."[238]

Some exegetes said this means "safe" from the Fire. It was also said to mean "safe" from the intentions of someone who would have attacked you outside the Sanctuary, and people sought refuge there during Jāhiliyyah. This is reflected in the statement of Allah Exalted, "And [remember] when We made the Sacred House a centre and a sanctuary for the people",[239] according to some interpretations.

It is reported that a group of people came to Saʿdūn al-Khawlānī in al-Munastīr[240]. They informed him that the Kutāmah[241] had killed a man, and that they had burned him on a fire for an entire night, but that it had done nothing to him and his body had remained white. "Perhaps he had performed Hajj three times?" Saʿdūn asked.

"Yes", they replied.

He said: "It was narrated to me that whoever performs Hajj once has fulfilled the obligation, whoever performs Hajj a second time lends his Lord a loan, and whoever performs Hajj three times, Allah will make his hair and body impermissible to the Fire."

When the Messenger of Allah ﷺ looked at the Kaʿbah, he said: "Welcome to you, house. How great you are! How great is your sanctity!"[242]

Ḥibbān in *Mawārid al-Ẓamʾān* (1031), where its referencing can be found.

238 *Āl ʿImrān*, 96-97.

239 *al-Baqarah*, 125.

240 A town in the east of Tunisia still known by the same name today.

241 A Berber tribe that lives in the north of the Kingdom of Morocco.

242 Related by Ṭabarānī in *Al-Kabīr* from Ibn ʿAbbās. Haythamī said in *Majmaʿ al-Zawāʾid* (3/292): "Its chain contains al-Ḥasan ibn Abī Jaʿfar. He is a weak narrator, although some said he is reliable." Attributed by Suyūṭī in *Al-Manāhil*, p. 1151, to Ṭabarānī in *Al-Awsaṭ* from Ibn ʿUmar and Jābir. Also reported by Tirmidhī (2032) in a *mawqūf* narration from Ibn ʿUmar. Tirmidhī said: "This hadith is *ḥasan gharīb*."

In another hadith, the Prophet ﷺ was reported to have said: "Anyone who supplicates to Allah Exalted at the black corner[243], Allah will respond to them, and likewise at the spout (*mīzāb*)[244]."[245]

And in another, he said: "Whoever performs two units of prayer behind the station [of Ibrāhīm] will be forgiven for their past and future shortcomings and will be gathered amongst those who are safe and secure on the Day of Judgement."[246]

I recited [the following hadith] to Qāḍī Abū ʿAlī. I said to him: "Abū al-ʿAbbās al-ʿUdhrī narrated to you from Abū Usāmah Muhammad ibn Aḥmad ibn Muhammad al-Harawī, [who] narrated to us from al-Ḥasan ibn Rashīq, who heard from Abū al-Ḥasan Muhammad ibn al-Ḥasan ibn Rāshid, who heard from Abū Bakr Muhammad ibn Idrīs, who heard from al-Ḥumaydī, who heard from Sufyān ibn ʿUyaynah, who heard from ʿAmr ibn Dīnār, who heard Ibn ʿAbbās say: 'I heard the Messenger of Allah ﷺ say: "No-one supplicates for something at this place of clinging (*multazam*) except that it is answered for them."'"[247]

---

243 i.e., the corner with the black stone.

244 The spout is located on the northern face of the Kaʿbah and flows onto the Stone of Ismāʿīl. The spout that exists today was built in Constantinople in 1276 AH by Sultan ʿAbd al-Majīd Khān and was erected that same year, and it is plated in roughly fifty *raṭl*s of gold. See *Riḥāb al-Bayt*, p. 182.

245 Related by Suyūṭī in *Al-Manāhil*, p. 1152, without mentioning its reference. Also related by al-Azraqī in *Tārīkh Makkah* (1/318) in a *mawqūf* narration from ʿAṭā, [with the wording]: "Whoever stands beneath the spout of the Kaʿbah and supplicates will be responded to and will emerge free from their sins like the day their mother gave birth to them." See also the chapter on the *adhkār* of circumambulation in Nawawī's *Al-Adhkār*.

246 Reported by Bukhārī (3544) and Muslim (2343).

247 Reported by Daylamī in *Musnad al-Firdaws* and Abū al-Fayḍ al-Fādānī in *Al-ʿUjālah fī al-Aḥādīth al-Musalsalah* (22) from Muhammad ibn al-Ḥasan ibn Rāshid with this *musalsal* chain. Graded *ḥasan* by Abū Bakr ibn Masdī, as found in *Al-ʿUjālah*. Dhahabī declared the narration fabricated in *Al-Mīzān* (in the biography of Muhammad ibn al-Ḥasan ibn ʿAlī ibn Rāshid al-Anṣārī), and Ibn Ḥajar concurred in *Lisān al-Mīzān*. Reported in a similar form by Saʿīd ibn Manṣūr (as found in *Al-Manāhil*, p. 1154) and by Bayhaqī in *Al-Sunan al-Kubrā* (5/164), in a *mawqūf* narration from Ibn ʿAbbās. He says in *Al-Jiyād*: "It is a strong evidence." I did not find the narration in Ḥusayn Asad's commentary of *Musnad al-Ḥumaydī*.

Ibn ʿAbbās said: "And I have not supplicated Allah for anything at this *multazam* since I heard this from the Messenger of Allah ﷺ except that it has been granted to me."

ʿAmr ibn Dīnār said: "And I have not supplicated Allah Exalted for anything at this *multazam* since I heard this from Ibn ʿAbbās except that it has been granted to me."

Sufyān said: "And I have not supplicated Allah for anything at this *multazam* since I heard this from ʿAmr ibn Dīnār except that it has been granted to me."

Al-Ḥumaydī said: "And I have not supplicated Allah for anything at this *multazam* since I heard this from Sufyān except that it has been granted to me."

Muhammad ibn Idrīs said: "And I have not supplicated Allah for anything at this *multazam* since I heard this from al-Ḥumaydī except that it has been granted to me."

Abū al-Ḥasan Muhammad ibn al-Ḥasan said: "And I have not supplicated Allah for anything at this *multazam* since I heard this from Muhammad ibn Idrīs except that it has been granted to me."

Abū Usāmah said: "I do not remember al-Ḥasan ibn Rashīq saying anything about it, but I have not supplicated Allah for anything from the affairs of this world at this *multazam* since I heard this from al-Ḥasan ibn Rashīq except that it has been granted to me, and I hope that the affairs of the Hereafter will also be granted to me."

Al-ʿUdhrī said: "And I have not supplicated Allah for anything at this *multazam* since I heard this from Abū Usāmah except that it has been granted to me."

Abū ʿAlī said: "I have supplicated Allah for many things, and some of them have been granted to me, and I hope from the vastness of His Grace that the rest of them will also be granted to me."

We have mentioned a few snippets that are not directly related to this chapter because of their connection to the previous chapter and in order to ensure maximum benefit, and Allah is the One Who guides to what is correct by His Mercy.

www.ingramcontent.com/pod-product-compliance
Lightning Source LLC
Chambersburg PA
CBHW031818110426
42743CB00057B/874
* 9 7 8 1 9 6 6 3 2 9 7 0 1 *